Allan's Wife

By

H. Rider Haggard

DEDICATION

My Dear Macumazahn,

It was your native name which I borrowed at the christening
of that Allen who has become as well known to me as any
other friend I have. It is therefore fitting that I should
dedicate to you this, his last tale--the story of his wife,
and the history of some further adventures which befell him.
They will remind you of many an African yarn--that with the
baboons may recall an experience of your own which I did not
share. And perhaps they will do more than this. Perhaps they
will bring back to you some of the long past romance of days
that are lost to us. The country of which Allan Quatermain
tells his tale is now, for the most part, as well known and
explored as are the fields of Norfolk. Where we shot and
trekked and galloped, scarcely seeing the face of civilized
man, there the gold-seeker builds his cities. The shadow of
the flag of Britain has, for a while, ceased to fall on the
Transvaal plains; the game has gone; the misty charm of the
morning has become the glare of day. All is changed. The
blue gums that we planted in the garden of the "Palatial"
must be large trees by now, and the "Palatial" itself has
passed from us. Jess sat in it waiting for her love after we
were gone. There she nursed him back to life. But Jess is

2

dead, and strangers own it, or perhaps it is a ruin.

For us too, Macumazahn, as for the land we loved, the mystery and promise of the morning are outworn; the mid-day sun burns overhead, and at times the way is weary. Few of those we knew are left. Some are victims to battle and murder, their bones strew the veldt; death has taken some in a more gentle fashion; others are hidden from us, we know not where. We might well fear to return to that land lest we also should see ghosts. But though we walk apart to-day, the past yet looks upon us with its unalterable eyes. Still we can remember many a boyish enterprise and adventure, lightly undertaken, which now would strike us as hazardous indeed. Still we can recall the long familiar line of the Pretoria Horse, the face of war and panic, the weariness of midnight patrols; aye, and hear the roar of guns echoed from the Shameful Hill.

To you then, Macumazahn, in perpetual memory of those eventful years of youth which we passed together in the African towns and on the African veldt, I dedicate these pages, subscribing myself now as always,

Your sincere friend,

Indanda.

To Arthur H. D. Cochrane, Esq.

ALLAN'S WIFE

CHAPTER I

EARLY DAYS

It may be remembered that in the last pages of his diary, written just before his death, Allan Quatermain makes allusion to his long dead wife, stating that he has written of her fully elsewhere.

When his death was known, his papers were handed to myself as his literary executor. Among them I found two manuscripts, of which the following is one. The other is simply a record of events wherein Mr. Quatermain was not personally concerned--a Zulu novel, the story of which was told to him by the hero many years after the tragedy had occurred. But with this we have nothing to do at present.

I have often thought (Mr. Quatermain's manuscript begins) that I would set down on paper the events connected with my marriage, and the loss of my most dear wife. Many years have now passed since that event, and to some extent time has softened the old grief, though Heaven knows it is still keen enough. On two or three occasions I have even begun the record. Once I gave it up because the writing of it depressed me beyond bearing, once because I was suddenly called away upon a journey, and the third time because a Kaffir boy found my manuscript convenient for lighting the kitchen fire.

But now that I am at leisure here in England, I will make a fourth attempt. If I succeed, the story may serve to interest some one in after years when I am dead and gone; before that I should not wish it to be published. It is a wild tale enough, and suggests some curious reflections.

I am the son of a missionary. My father was originally curate in charge of a small parish in Oxfordshire. He had already been some ten years married to my dear mother when he went there, and he had four children, of whom I was the youngest. I remember faintly the place where we lived. It was an ancient long grey house, facing the road. There was a very large tree of some sort in the garden. It was hollow, and we children used to play about inside of it, and knock knots of wood from the rough bark. We all slept in a kind of attic, and my mother always came and kissed us when we were in bed. I used to wake up and see her bending over me, a candle in her hand. There was a curious kind of pole projecting from the wall over my bed. Once I was dreadfully frightened because my eldest brother made me hang to it by my hands. That is all I remember about our old home. It has been pulled down long ago, or I would journey there to see it.

A little further down the road was a large house with big iron gates to it, and on the top of the gate pillars sat two stone lions, which were so hideous that I was afraid of them. Perhaps this sentiment was prophetic. One could see the house by peeping through the bars of the gates. It was a gloomy-looking place, with a tall yew hedge round it; but in the summer-time some flowers grew about the sun-dial in the grass plat. This house was called the Hall, and Squire Carson lived there. One Christmas--it must have been the Christmas before my father emigrated, or I should not remember it--we children went to a Christmas-tree festivity at the Hall. There was a great party there, and footmen wearing red waistcoats stood at the door. In the dining-room, which was panelled with black oak, was the Christmas-tree. Squire Carson stood in front of it. He was a tall, dark man, very quiet in his manners, and he wore a bunch of seals on his waistcoat. We used to think him old, but as a matter of fact he was then not more than forty. He had been, as I afterwards learned, a great traveller in his youth, and some six or seven years before this date he married a lady who was half a Spaniard--a papist, my father called her. I can remember her well. She was small and very pretty, with a rounded figure, large black eyes, and glittering teeth. She spoke English with a curious accent. I suppose that I must have been a funny child to look at, and I know that my hair stood up on my head then as it does now, for I still have a sketch of myself that my mother made of me, in which this peculiarity is strongly marked. On this occasion of the Christmas-tree I remember that Mrs. Carson turned to a tall, foreign-looking gentleman who stood beside her, and, tapping him affectionately on the shoulder with her gold eye-glasses, said--

7

"Look, cousin--look at that droll little boy with the big brown eyes; his hair is like a--what you call him?--scrubbing-brush. Oh, what a droll little boy!"

The tall gentleman pulled at his moustache, and, taking Mrs. Carson's hand in his, began to smooth my hair down with it till I heard her whisper--

"Leave go my hand, cousin. Thomas is looking like--like the thunderstorm."

Thomas was the name of Mr. Carson, her husband.

After that I hid myself as well as I could behind a chair, for I was shy, and watched little Stella Carson, who was the squire's only child, giving the children presents off the tree. She was dressed as Father Christmas, with some soft white stuff round her lovely little face, and she had large dark eyes, which I thought more beautiful than anything I had ever seen. At last it came to my turn to receive a present--oddly enough, considered in the light of future events, it was a large monkey. Stella reached it down from one of the lower boughs of the tree and handed it to me, saying--

"Dat is my Christmas present to you, little Allan Quatermain."

As she did so her sleeve, which was covered with cotton wool, spangled over with something that shone, touched one of the tapers and caught fire--how I do not know--and the flame ran up her arm towards her throat. She stood quite still. I suppose that she was paralysed with fear; and the ladies who were near screamed very loud, but did nothing. Then some impulse seized me--perhaps instinct would be a better word to use, considering my age. I threw myself upon the child, and, beating at the fire with my hands, mercifully succeeded in extinguishing it before it really got hold. My wrists were so badly scorched that they had to be wrapped up in wool for a long time afterwards, but with the exception of a single burn upon her throat, little Stella Carson was not much hurt.

This is all that I remember about the Christmas-tree at the Hall. What happened afterwards is lost to me, but to this day in my sleep I sometimes see little Stella's sweet face and the stare of terror in her dark eyes as the fire ran up her arm. This, however, is not wonderful, for I had, humanly speaking, saved the life of her who was destined to be my wife.

The next event which I can recall clearly is that my mother and three brothers all fell ill of fever, owing, as I afterwards learned, to the poisoning of our well by some evil-minded person, who threw a dead sheep into it.

It must have been while they were ill that Squire Carson came one day to the vicarage. The weather was still cold, for there was a fire in the study, and I sat before the fire writing letters on a piece of paper with a pencil, while my father walked up and down the room talking to himself. Afterwards I knew that he was praying for the lives of his wife and children. Presently a servant came to the door and said that some one wanted to see him.

"It is the squire, sir," said the maid, "and he says he particularly wishes to see you."

"Very well," answered my father, wearily, and presently Squire Carson came in. His face was white and haggard, and his eyes shone so fiercely that I was afraid of him.

"Forgive me for intruding on you at such a time, Quatermain," he said, in a hoarse voice, "but to-morrow I leave this place for ever, and I wish to speak to you before I go--indeed, I must speak to you."

"Shall I send Allan away?" said my father, pointing to me.

"No; let him bide. He will not understand." Nor, indeed, did I at the time, but I remembered every word, and in after years their meaning grew on me.

"First tell me," he went on, "how are they?" and he pointed upwards with his thumb.

"My wife and two of the boys are beyond hope," my father answered, with a groan. "I do not know how it will go with the third. The Lord's will be done!"

"The Lord's will be done," the squire echoed, solemnly. "And now, Quatermain, listen--my wife's gone."

"Gone!" my father answered. "Who with?"

"With that foreign cousin of hers. It seems from a letter she left me that she always cared for him, not for me. She married me because she thought me a rich English milord. Now she has run through my property, or most of it, and gone. I don't know where. Luckily, she did not care to encumber her new career with the child; Stella is left to me."

"That is what comes of marrying a papist, Carson," said my father. That was his fault; he was as good and charitable a man as ever lived, but he was bigoted. "What are you going to do--follow her?"

He laughed bitterly in answer.

"Follow her!" he said; "why should I follow her? If I met her I might kill her or him, or both of them, because of the disgrace they have brought upon my child's name. No, I never want to look upon her face again. I trusted her, I tell you, and she has betrayed me. Let her go and find her fate. But I am going too. I am weary of my life."

11

"Surely, Carson, surely," said my father, "you do not mean----"

"No, no; not that. Death comes soon enough. But I will leave this civilized world which is a lie. We will go right away into the wilds, I and my child, and hide our shame. Where? I don't know where. Anywhere, so long as there are no white faces, no smooth educated tongues----"

"You are mad, Carson," my father answered. "How will you live? How can you educate Stella? Be a man and wear it down."

"I will be a man, and I will wear it down, but not here, Quatermain. Education! Was not she--that woman who was my wife--was not she highly educated?--the cleverest woman in the country forsooth. Too clever for me, Quatermain--too clever by half! No, no, Stella shall be brought up in a different school; if it be possible, she shall forget her very name. Good-bye, old friend, good-bye for ever. Do not try to find me out, henceforth I shall be like one dead to you, to you and all I knew," and he was gone.

"Mad," said my father, with a heavy sigh. "His trouble has turned his brain. But he will think better of it."

At that moment the nurse came hurrying in and whispered something in his ear. My father's face turned deadly pale. He clutched at the table to support himself, then staggered from the room. My mother was dying!

12

It was some days afterwards, I do not know exactly how long, that my
father took me by the hand and led me upstairs into the big room which
had been my mother's bedroom. There she lay, dead in her coffin, with
flowers in her hand. Along the wall of the room were arranged three
little white beds, and on each of the beds lay one of my brothers. They
all looked as though they were asleep, and they all had flowers in their
hands. My father told me to kiss them, because I should not see them any
more, and I did so, though I was very frightened. I did not know why.
Then he took me in his arms and kissed me.

"The Lord hath given," he said, "and the Lord hath taken away; blessed
be the name of the Lord."

I cried very much, and he took me downstairs, and after that I have only
a confused memory of men dressed in black carrying heavy burdens towards
the grey churchyard!

Next comes a vision of a great ship and wide tossing waters. My father
could no longer bear to live in England after the loss that had fallen
on him, and made up his mind to emigrate to South Africa. We must have
been poor at the time--indeed, I believe that a large portion of
our income went from my father on my mother's death. At any rate we
travelled with the steerage passengers, and the intense discomfort of
the journey with the rough ways of our fellow emigrants still remain
upon my mind. At last it came to an end, and we reached Africa, which I

was not to leave again for many, many years.

In those days civilization had not made any great progress in Southern Africa. My father went up the country and became a missionary among the Kaffirs, near to where the town of Cradock now stands, and here I grew to manhood. There were a few Boer farmers in the neighbourhood, and gradually a little settlement of whites gathered round our mission station--a drunken Scotch blacksmith and wheelwright was about the most interesting character, who, when he was sober, could quote the Scottish poet Burns and the Ingoldsby Legends, then recently published, literally by the page. It was from that I contracted a fondness for the latter amusing writings, which has never left me. Burns I never cared for so much, probably because of the Scottish dialect which repelled me. What little education I got was from my father, but I never had much leaning towards books, nor he much time to teach them to me. On the other hand, I was always a keen observer of the ways of men and nature. By the time that I was twenty I could speak Dutch and three or four Kaffir dialects perfectly, and I doubt if there was anybody in South Africa who understood native ways of thought and action more completely than I did. Also I was really a very good shot and horseman, and I think--as, indeed, my subsequent career proves to have been the case--a great deal tougher than the majority of men. Though I was then, as now, light and small, nothing seemed to tire me. I could bear any amount of exposure and privation, and I never met the native who was my master in feats of endurance. Of course, all that is different now, I am speaking of my early manhood.

14

It may be wondered that I did not run absolutely wild in such surroundings, but I was held back from this by my father's society. He was one of the gentlest and most refined men that I ever met; even the most savage Kaffir loved him, and his influence was a very good one for me. He used to call himself one of the world's failures. Would that there were more such failures. Every morning when his work was done he would take his prayer-book and, sitting on the little stoep or verandah of our station, would read the evening psalms to himself. Sometimes there was not light enough for this, but it made no difference, he knew them all by heart. When he had finished he would look out across the cultivated lands where the mission Kaffirs had their huts.

But I knew it was not these he saw, but rather the grey English church, and the graves ranged side by side before the yew near the wicket gate.

It was there on the stoep that he died. He had not been well, and one evening I was talking to him, and his mind went back to Oxfordshire and my mother. He spoke of her a good deal, saying that she had never been out of his mind for a single day during all these years, and that he rejoiced to think he was drawing near that land wither she had gone. Then he asked me if I remembered the night when Squire Carson came into the study at the vicarage, and told him that his wife had run away, and that he was going to change his name and bury himself in some remote land.

15

I answered that I remembered it perfectly.

"I wonder where he went to," said my father, "and if he and his daughter Stella are still alive. Well, well! I shall never meet them again. But life is a strange thing, Allan, and you may. If you ever do, give them my kind love."

After that I left him. We had been suffering more than usual from the depredations of the Kaffir thieves, who stole our sheep at night, and, as I had done before, and not without success, I determined to watch the kraal and see if I could catch them. Indeed, it was from this habit of mine of watching at night that I first got my native name of Macumazahn, which may be roughly translated as "he who sleeps with one eye open." So I took my rifle and rose to go. But he called me to him and kissed me on the forehead, saying, "God bless you, Allan! I hope that you will think of your old father sometimes, and that you will lead a good and happy life."

I remember that I did not much like his tone at the time, but set it down to an attack of low spirits, to which he grew very subject as the years went on. I went down to the kraal and watched till within an hour of sunrise; then, as no thieves appeared, returned to the station. As I came near I was astonished to see a figure sitting in my father's chair. At first I thought it must be a drunken Kaffir, then that my father had fallen asleep there.

And so he had,--for he was dead!

CHAPTER II

THE FIRE-FIGHT

When I had buried my father, and seen a successor installed in his place--for the station was the property of the Society--I set to work to carry out a plan which I had long cherished, but been unable to execute because it would have involved separation from my father. Put shortly, it was to undertake a trading journey of exploration right through the countries now known as the Free State and the Transvaal, and as much further North as I could go. It was an adventurous scheme, for though the emigrant Boers had begun to occupy positions in these territories, they were still to all practical purposes unexplored. But I was now alone in the world, and it mattered little what became of me; so, driven on by the overmastering love of adventure, which, old as I am, will perhaps still be the cause of my death, I determined to undertake the journey.

Accordingly I sold such stock and goods as we had upon the station, reserving only the two best waggons and two spans of oxen. The proceeds I invested in such goods as were then in fashion, for trading purposes, and in guns and ammunition. The guns would have moved any modern explorer to merriment; but such as they were I managed to do a good deal of execution with them. One of them was a single-barrelled, smooth bore, fitted for percussion caps--a roer we called it--which threw a three-ounce ball, and was charged with a handful of coarse black powder.

Many is the elephant that I killed with that roer, although it generally knocked me backwards when I fired it, which I only did under compulsion. The best of the lot, perhaps, was a double-barrelled No. 12 shot-gun, but it had flint locks. Also there were some old tower muskets, which might or might not throw straight at seventy yards. I took six Kaffirs with me, and three good horses, which were supposed to be salted--that is, proof against the sickness. Among the Kaffirs was an old fellow named Indaba-zimbi, which, being translated, means "tongue of iron." I suppose he got this name from his strident voice and exhaustless eloquence. This man was a great character in his way. He had been a noted witch-doctor among a neighbouring tribe, and came to the station under the following circumstances, which, as he plays a considerable part in this history, are perhaps worth recording.

Two years before my father's death I had occasion to search the country round for some lost oxen. After a long and useless quest it occurred to me that I had better go to the place where the oxen were bred by a Kaffir chief, whose name I forget, but whose kraal was about fifty miles from our station. There I journeyed, and found the oxen safe at home. The chief entertained me handsomely, and on the following morning I went to pay my respects to him before leaving, and was somewhat surprised to find a collection of some hundreds of men and women sitting round him anxiously watching the sky in which the thunder-clouds were banking up in a very ominous way.

"You had better wait, white man," said the chief, "and see the rain-doctors fight the lightning."

I inquired what he meant, and learned that this man, Indaba-zimbi, had
for some years occupied the position of wizard-in-chief to the tribe,
although he was not a member of it, having been born in the country now
known as Zululand. But a son of the chief's, a man of about thirty,
had lately set up as a rival in supernatural powers. This irritated
Indaba-zimbi beyond measure, and a quarrel ensued between the two
witch-doctors that resulted in a challenge to trial by lightning being
given and accepted. These were the conditions. The rivals must await the
coming of a serious thunderstorm, no ordinary tempest would serve their
turn. Then, carrying assegais in their hands, they must take their stand
within fifty paces of each other upon a certain patch of ground where
the big thunderbolts were observed to strike continually, and by the
exercise of their occult powers and invocations to the lightning, must
strive to avert death from themselves and bring it on their rival. The
terms of this singular match had been arranged a month previously,
but no storm worthy of the occasion had arisen. Now the local
weather-prophets believed it to be brewing.

I inquired what would happen if neither of the men were struck, and was
told that they must then wait for another storm. If they escaped the
second time, however, they would be held to be equal in power, and be
jointly consulted by the tribe upon occasions of importance.

The prospect of being a spectator of so unusual a sight overcame my

20

desire to be gone, and I accepted the chief's invitation to see it

out. Before mid-day I regretted it, for though the western heavens grew

darker and darker, and the still air heralded the coming of the storm,

yet it did not come. By four o'clock, however, it became obvious that

it must burst soon--at sunset, the old chief said, and in the company

of the whole assembly I moved down to the place of combat. The kraal was

built on the top of a hill, and below it the land sloped gently to the

banks of a river about half a mile away. On the hither side of the

bank was the piece of land that was, the natives said, "loved of the

lightning." Here the magicians took up their stand, while the spectators

grouped themselves on the hillside about two hundred yards away--which

was, I thought, rather too near to be pleasant. When we had sat there

for a while my curiosity overcame me, and I asked leave of the chief to

go down and inspect the arena. He said I might do so at my own risk. I

told him that the fire from above would not hurt white men, and went

to find that the spot was a bed of iron ore, thinly covered with grass,

which of course accounted for its attracting the lightning from the

storms as they travelled along the line of the river. At each end of

this iron-stone area were placed the combatants, Indaba-zimbi facing the

east, and his rival the west, and before each there burned a little

fire made of some scented root. Moreover they were dressed in all the

paraphernalia of their craft, snakeskins, fish-bladders, and I know not

what beside, while round their necks hung circlets of baboons' teeth

and bones from human hands. First I went to the western end where

the chief's son stood. He was pointing with his assegai towards the

advancing storm, and invoking it in a voice of great excitement.

21

"Come, fire, and lick up Indaba-zimbi!

"Hear me, Storm Devil, and lick Indaba-zimbi with your red tongue!

"Spit on him with your rain!

"Whirl him away in your breath!

"Make him as nothing--melt the marrow in his bones!

"Run into his heart and burn away the lies!

"Show all the people who is the true Witch Finder!

"Let me not be put to shame in the eyes of this white man!"

Thus he spoke, or rather chanted, and all the while rubbed his broad chest--for he was a very fine man--with some filthy compound of medicine or mouti.

After a while, getting tired of his song, I walked across the iron-stone, to where Indaba-zimbi sat by his fire. He was not chanting at all, but his performance was much more impressive. It consisted in staring at the eastern sky, which was perfectly clear of cloud, and every now and again beckoning at it with his finger, then turning round to point with the assegai towards his rival. For a while I looked at him in silence. He was a curious wizened man, apparently over fifty years of age, with thin hands that looked as tough as wire. His nose was much sharper than is usual among these races, and he had a queer habit of holding his head sideways like a bird when he spoke, which, in addition to the humour that lurked in his eye, gave him a most comical appearance. Another strange thing about him was that he had a single white lock of hair among his black wool. At last I spoke to him:

"Indaba-zimbi, my friend," I said, "you may be a good witch-doctor, but you are certainly a fool. It is no good beckoning at the blue sky while your enemy is getting a start with the storm."

"You may be clever, but don't think you know everything, white man," the old fellow answered, in a high, cracked voice, and with something like a grin.

"They call you Iron-tongue," I went on; "you had better use it, or the Storm Devil won't hear you."

"The fire from above runs down iron," he answered, "so I keep my tongue quiet. Oh, yes, let him curse away, I'll put him out presently. Look now, white man."

I looked, and in the eastern sky there grew a cloud. At first it was small, though very black, but it gathered with extraordinary rapidity.

This was odd enough, but as I had seen the same thing happen before it did not particularly astonish me. It is by no means unusual in Africa for two thunderstorms to come up at the same time from different points of the compass.

"You had better get on, Indaba-zimbi," I said, "the big storm is coming along fast, and will soon eat up that baby of yours," and I pointed to the west.

"Babies sometimes grow to giants, white man," said Indaba-zimbi, beckoning away vigorously. "Look now at my cloud-child."

I looked; the eastern storm was spreading itself from earth to sky, and in shape resembled an enormous man. There was its head, its shoulders, and its legs; yes, it was like a huge giant travelling across the heavens. The light of the setting sun escaping from beneath the lower edge of the western storm shot across the intervening space in a sheet of splendour, and, lighting upon the advancing figure of cloud, wrapped its middle in hues of glory too wonderful to be described; but beneath and above this glowing belt his feet and head were black as jet. Presently, as I watched, an awful flash of light shot from the head of the cloud, circled it about as though with a crown of living fire, and vanished.

"Aha," chuckled old Indaba-zimbi, "my little boy is putting on his man's ring," and he tapped the gum ring on his own head, which natives assume when they reach a certain age and dignity. "Now, white man, unless you are a bigger wizard than either of us you had better clear off, for the fire-fight is about to begin."

I thought this sound advice.

"Good luck go with you, my black uncle," I said. "I hope you don't feel the iniquities of a mis-spent life weighing on you at the last."

"You look after yourself, and think of your own sins, young man," he answered, with a grim smile, and taking a pinch of snuff, while at that very moment a flash of lightning, I don't know from which storm, struck the ground within thirty paces of me. That was enough for me, I took to my heels, and as I went I heard old Indaba-zimbi's dry chuckle of amusement.

I climbed the hill till I came to where the chief was sitting with his indunas, or headmen, and sat down near to him. I looked at the man's face and saw that he was intensely anxious for his son's safety, and by no means confident of the young man's powers to resist the magic of Indaba-zimbi. He was talking in a low voice to the induna next to him. I affected to take no notice and to be concentrating my attention on the novel scene before me; but in those days I had very quick ears, and caught the drift of the conversation.

"Hearken!" the chief was saying, "if the magic of Indaba-zimbi prevails against my son I will endure him no more. Of this I am sure, that when he has slain my son he will slay me, me also, and make himself chief in my place. I fear Indaba-zimbi. Ou!"

"Black One," answered the induna, "wizards die as dogs die, and, once dead, dogs bark no more."

"And once dead," said the chiefs, "wizards work no more spells," and he bent and whispered in the induna's ear, looking at the assegai in his hand as he whispered.

"Good, my father, good!" said the induna, presently. "It shall be done to-night, if the lightning does not do it first."

"A bad look-out for old Indaba-zimbi," I said to myself. "They mean to kill him." Then I thought no more of the matter for a while, the scene before me was too tremendous.

The two storms were rapidly rushing together. Between them was a gulf of blue sky, and from time to time flashes of blinding light passed across this gulf, leaping from cloud to cloud. I remember that they reminded me of the story of the heathen god Jove and his thunderbolts. The storm that was shaped like a giant and ringed with the glory of the sinking sun made an excellent Jove, and I am sure that the bolts which leapt from it could not have been surpassed even in mythological times.

26

Oddly enough, as yet the flashes were not followed by thunder. A deadly stillness lay upon the place, the cattle stood silently on the hillside, even the natives were awed to silence. Dark shadows crept along the bosom of the hills, the river to the right and left was hidden in wreaths of cloud, but before us and beyond the combatants it shone like a line of silver beneath the narrowing space of open sky. Now the western tempest was scrawled all over with lines of intolerable light, while the inky head of the cloud-giant to the east was continually suffused with a white and deadly glow that came and went in pulses, as though a blood of flame was being pumped into it from the heart of the storm.

The silence deepened and deepened, the shadows grew blacker and blacker, then suddenly all nature began to moan beneath the breath of an icy wind. On sped the wind; the smooth surface of the river was ruffled by it into little waves, the tall grass bowed low before it, and in its wake came the hissing sound of furious rain.

Ah! the storms had met. From each there burst an awful blaze of dazzling flame, and now the hill on which we sat rocked at the noise of the following thunder. The light went out of the sky, darkness fell suddenly on the land, but not for long. Presently the whole landscape grew vivid in the flashes, it appeared and disappeared, now everything was visible for miles, now even the men at my side vanished in the blackness. The thunder rolled and cracked and pealed like the trump of doom, whirlwinds tore round, lifting dust and even stones high into the air, and in a

27

low, continuous undertone rose the hiss of the rushing rain.

I put my hand before my eyes to shield them from the terrible glare, and looked beneath it towards the lists of iron-stone. As flash followed flash, from time to time I caught sight of the two wizards. They were slowly advancing towards one another, each pointing at his foe with the assegai in his hand. I could see their every movement, and it seemed to me that the chain lightning was striking the iron-stone all round them.

Suddenly the thunder and lightning ceased for a minute, everything grew black, and, except for the rain, silent.

"It is over one way or the other, chief," I called out into the darkness.

"Wait, white man, wait!" answered the chief, in a voice thick with anxiety and fear.

Hardly were the words out of his mouth when the heavens were lit up again till they literally seemed to flame. There were the men, not ten paces apart. A great flash fell between them, I saw them stagger beneath the shock. Indaba-zimbi recovered himself first--at any rate when the next flash came he was standing bolt upright, pointing with his assegai towards his enemy. The chief's son was still on his legs, but he was staggering like a drunken man, and the assegai had fallen from his hand.

Darkness! then again a flash, more fearful, if possible, than any that had gone before. To me it seemed to come from the east, right over the head of Indaba-zimbi. At that instant I saw the chief's son wrapped, as it were, in the heart of it. Then the thunder pealed, the rain burst over us like a torrent, and I saw no more.

The worst of the storm was done, but for a while the darkness was so dense that we could not move, nor, indeed, was I inclined to leave the safety of the hillside where the lightning was never known to strike, and venture down to the iron-stone. Occasionally there still came flashes, but, search as we would, we could see no trace of either of the wizards. For my part, I believed that they were both dead. Now the clouds slowly rolled away down the course of the river, and with them went the rain; and now the stars shone in their wake.

"Let us go and see," said the old chief, rising and shaking the water from his hair. "The fire-fight is ended, let us go and see who has conquered."

I rose and followed him, dripping as though I had swum a hundred yards with my clothes on, and after me came all the people of the kraal.

We reached the spot; even in that light I could see where the iron-stone had been split and fused by the thunderbolts. While I was staring about me, I suddenly heard the chief, who was on my right, give a low moan, and saw the people cluster round him. I went up and looked. There, on

29

the ground, lay the body of his son. It was a dreadful sight. The hair was burnt off his head, the copper rings upon his arms were fused, the assegai handle which lay near was literally shivered into threads, and, when I took hold of his arm, it seemed to me that every bone of it was broken.

The men with the chief stood gazing silently, while the women wailed.

"Great is the magic of Indaba-zimbi!" said a man, at length. The chief turned and struck him a heavy blow with the kerrie in his hand.

"Great or not, thou dog, he shall die," he cried, "and so shalt thou if thou singest his praises so loudly."

I said nothing, but thinking it probable that Indaba-zimbi had shared the fate of his enemy, I went to look. But I could see nothing of him, and at length, being thoroughly chilled with the wet, started back to my waggon to change my clothes. On reaching it, I was rather surprised to see a strange Kaffir seated on the driving-box wrapped up in a blanket.

"Hullo! come out of that," I said.

The figure on the box slowly unrolled the blanket, and with great deliberation took a pinch of snuff.

"It was a good fire-fight, white man, was it not?" said Indaba-zimbi, in his high, cracked voice. "But he never had a chance against me, poor boy. He knew nothing about it. See, white man, what becomes of presumption in the young. It is sad, very sad, but I made the flashes fly, didn't I?"

"You old humbug," I said, "unless you are careful you will soon learn what comes of presumption in the old, for your chief is after you with an assegai, and it will take all your magic to dodge that."

"Now you don't say so," said Indaba-zimbi, clambering off the waggon with rapidity; "and all because of this wretched upstart. There's gratitude for you, white man. I expose him, and they want to kill me. Well, thank you for the hint. We shall meet again before long," and he was gone like a shot, and not too soon, for just then some of the chief's men came up to the waggon.

On the following morning I started homewards. The first face I saw on arriving at the station was that of Indaba-zimbi.

"How do you do, Macumazahn?" he said, holding his head on one side and nodding his white lock. "I hear you are Christians here, and I want to try a new religion. Mine must be a bad one seeing that my people wanted to kill me for exposing an impostor."

31

CHAPTER III

NORTHWARDS

I make no apology to myself, or to anybody who may happen to read this
narrative in future, for having set out the manner of my meeting with
Indaba-zimbi: first, because it was curious, and secondly, because he
takes some hand in the subsequent events. If that old man was a
humbug, he was a very clever one. What amount of truth there was in his
pretensions to supernatural powers it is not for me to determine, though
I may have my own opinion on the subject. But there was no mistake as to
the extraordinary influence he exercised over his fellow-natives. Also
he quite got round my poor father. At first the old gentleman declined
to have him at the station, for he had a great horror of these Kaffir
wizards or witch-finders. But Indaba-zimbi persuaded him that he was
anxious to investigate the truths of Christianity, and challenged him to
a discussion. The argument lasted two years--to the time of my father's
death, indeed. At the conclusion of each stage Indaba-zimbi would
remark, in the words of the Roman Governor, "Almost, praying white man,
thou persuadest me to become a Christian," but he never quite became
one--indeed, I do not think he ever meant to. It was to him that my
father addressed his "Letters to a Native Doubter." This work, which,
unfortunately, remains in manuscript, is full of wise saws and learned
instances. It ought to be published together with a précis of the
doubter's answers, which were verbal.

So the talk went on. If my father had lived I believe it would be going on now, for both the disputants were quite inexhaustible. Meanwhile Indaba-zimbi was allowed to live on the station on condition that he practised no witchcraft, which my father firmly believed to be a wile of the devil. He said that he would not, but for all that there was never an ox lost, or a sudden death, but he was consulted by those interested.

When he had been with us a year, a deputation came to him from the tribe he had left, asking him to return. Things had not gone well with them since he went away, they said, and now the chief, his enemy, was dead. Old Indaba-zimbi listened to them till they had done, and, as he listened, raked sand into a little heap with his toes. Then he spoke, pointing to the little heap, "There is your tribe to-day," he said. Then he lifted his heel and stamped the heap flat. "There is your tribe before three moons are gone. Nothing is left of it. You drove me away: I will have no more to do with you; but when you are being killed think of my words."

The messengers went. Three months afterwards I heard that the whole community had been wiped out by an Impi of raiding Pondos.

When I was at length ready to start upon my expedition, I went to old Indaba-zimbi to say good-bye to him, and was rather surprised to find him engaged in rolling up medicine, assegais, and other sundries in his blankets.

33

"Good-bye, Indaba-zimbi," I said, "I am going to trek north."

"Yes, Macumazahn," he answered, with his head on one side; "and so am I--I want to see that country. We will go together."

"Will we!" I said; "wait till you are asked, you old humbug."

"You had better ask me, then, Macumazahn, for if you don't you will never come back alive. Now that the old chief (my father) is gone to where the storms come from," and he nodded to the sky, "I feel myself getting into bad habits again. So last night I just threw up the bones and worked out about your journey, and I can tell you this, that if you don't take me you will die, and, what is more, you will lose one who is dearer to you than life in a strange fashion. So just because you gave me that hint a couple of years ago, I made up my mind to come with you."

"Don't talk stuff to me," I said.

"Ah, very well, Macumazahn, very well; but what happened to my own people six months ago, and what did I tell the messengers would happen? They drove me away, and they are gone. If you drive me away you will soon be gone too," and he nodded his white lock at me and smiled. Now I was not more superstitious than other people, but somehow old Indaba-zimbi impressed me. Also I knew his extraordinary influence over every class of native, and bethought me that he might be useful in that way.

"All right," I said: "I appoint you witch-finder to the expedition without pay."

"First serve, then ask for wages," he answered. "I am glad to see that you have enough imagination not to be altogether a fool, like most white men, Macumazahn. Yes, yes, it is want of imagination that makes people fools; they won't believe what they can't understand. You can't understand my prophecies any more than the fool at the kraal could understand that I was his master with the lightning. Well, it is time to trek, but if I were you, Macumazahn, I should take one waggon, not two."

"Why?" I said.

"Because you will lose your waggons, and it is better to lose one than two."

"Oh, nonsense!" I said.

"All right, Macumazahn, live and learn." And without another word he walked to the foremost waggon, put his bundle into it, and climbed on to the front seat.

So having bid an affectionate adieu to my white friends, including the old Scotchman who got drunk in honour of the event, and quoted Burns till the tears ran down his face, at length I started, and travelled slowly northwards. For the first three weeks nothing very particular befell me. Such Kaffirs as we came in contact with were friendly, and game literally swarmed. Nobody living in those parts of South Africa nowadays can have the remotest idea of what the veldt was like even thirty years ago.

Often and often I have crept shivering on to my waggon-box just as the sun rose and looked out. At first one would see nothing but a vast field of white mist suffused towards the east by a tremulous golden glow, through which the tops of stony koppies stood up like gigantic beacons. From the dense mist would come strange sounds--snorts, gruntings, bellows, and the thunder of countless hoofs. Presently this great curtain would grow thinner, then it would melt, as the smoke from a pipe melts into the air, and for miles on miles the wide rolling country interspersed with bush opened to the view. But it was not tenantless as it is now, for as far as the eye could reach it would be literally black with game. Here to the right might be a herd of vilderbeeste that could not number less than two thousand. Some were grazing, some gambolled, whisking their white tails into the air, while all round the old bulls stood upon hillocks sniffing suspiciously at the breeze. There, in front, a hundred yards away, though to the unpractised eye they looked much closer, because of the dazzling clearness of the atmosphere, was a great herd of springbok trekking along in single file. Ah, they have come to the waggon-track and do not like the look of it. What will they do?--go back? Not a bit of it. It is nearly thirty feet wide, but that is nothing to a springbok. See, the first of them bounds into the air like a ball. How beautifully the sunshine gleams upon his golden hide! He has cleared it, and the others come after him in numberless succession, all except the fawns, who cannot jump so far, and have to scamper over the doubtful path with a terrified bah. What is that yonder, moving above the tops of the mimosa, in the little dell at the foot of the koppie? Giraffes, by George! three of them; there will be marrow-bones for supper to-night. Hark! the ground shakes behind us, and over the brow of the rise rush a vast herd of blesbock. On they come at full gallop, their long heads held low, they look like so many bearded goats. I thought so--behind them is a pack of wild dogs, their fur draggled, their tongues lolling. They are in full cry; the giraffes hear them and are away, rolling round the koppie like a ship in a heavy sea. No marrow-bones after all. See! the foremost dogs are close on a buck. He has galloped far and is outworn. One springs at his flank and misses him. The buck gives a kind of groan, looks wildly round and sees the waggon. He seems to hesitate a moment, then in his despair rushes up to it, and falls exhausted among the oxen. The dogs pull up some thirty paces away, panting and snarling. Now, boy, the gun--no, not the rifle, the shot-gun loaded with loopers.

Bang! bang! there, my friends, two of you will never hunt buck again. No, don't touch the buck, for he has come to us for shelter, and he shall have it.

Ah, how beautiful is nature before man comes to spoil it!

Such a sight as this have I seen many a hundred times, and I hope to see it again before I die.

The first real adventure that befell me on this particular journey was with elephants, which I will relate because of its curious termination. Just before we crossed the Orange River we came to a stretch of forest-land some twenty miles broad. The night we entered this forest we camped in a lovely open glade. A few yards ahead tambouki grass was growing to the height of a man, or rather it had been; now, with the exception of a few stalks here and there, it was crushed quite flat. It was already dusk when we camped; but after the moon got up I walked from the fire to see how this had happened. One glance was enough for me; a great herd of elephants had evidently passed over the tall grass not many hours before. The sight of their spoor rejoiced me exceedingly, for though I had seen wild elephants, at that time I had never shot one. Moreover, the sight of elephant spoor to the African hunter is what "colour in the pan" is to the prospector of gold. It is by the ivory that he lives, and to shoot it or trade it is his chief aim in life. My resolution was soon taken. I would camp the waggons for a while in the forest, and start on horseback after the elephants.

I communicated my decision to Indaba-zimbi and the other Kaffirs. The latter were not loth, for your Kaffir loves hunting, which means plenty of meat and congenial occupation, but Indaba-zimbi would express no opinion. I saw him retire to a little fire that he had lit for himself, and go through some mysterious performances with bones and clay mixed

38

with ashes, which were watched with the greatest interest by the other Kaffirs. At length he rose, and, coming forward, informed me that it was all right, and that I did well to go and hunt the elephants, as I should get plenty of ivory; but he advised me to go on foot. I said I should do nothing of the sort, but meant to ride. I am wiser now; this was the first and last time that I ever attempted to hunt elephants on horseback.

Accordingly we started at dawn, I, Indaba-zimbi, and three men; the rest I left with the waggons. I was on horseback, and so was my driver, a good rider and a skilful shot for a Kaffir, but Indaba-zimbi and the others walked. From dawn till mid-day we followed the trail of the herd, which was as plain as a high road. Then we off-saddled to let the horses rest and feed, and about three o'clock started on again. Another hour or so passed, and still there was no sign of elephants. Evidently the herd had travelled fast and far, and I began to think that we should have to give it up, when suddenly I caught sight of a brown mass moving through the thorn-trees on the side of a slope about a quarter of a mile away. My heart seemed to jump into my mouth. Where is the hunter who has not felt like this at the sight of his first elephant?

I called a halt, and then the wind being right, we set to work to stalk the bull. Very quietly I rode down the hither side of the slope till we came to the bottom, which was densely covered with bush. Here I saw the elephants had been feeding, for broken branches and upturned trees lay all about. I did not take much notice, however, for all my thoughts

39

were fixed upon the bull I was stalking, when suddenly my horse gave a violent start that nearly threw me from the saddle, and there came a mighty rush and upheaval of something in front of me. I looked: there was the hinder part of a second bull elephant not four yards off. I could just catch sight of its outstretched ears projecting on either side. I had disturbed it sleeping, and it was running away.

Obviously the best thing to do would have been to let it run, but I was young in those days and foolish, and in the excitement of the moment I lifted my "roer" or elephant gun and fired at the great brute over my horse's head. The recoil of the heavy gun nearly knocked me off the horse. I recovered myself, however, and, as I did so, saw the bull lurch forward, for the impact of a three-ounce bullet in the flank will quicken the movement even of an elephant. By this time I had realized the folly of the shot, and devoutly hoped that the bull would take no further notice of it. But he took a different view of the matter. Pulling himself up in a series of plunges, he spun round and came for me with outstretched ears and uplifted trunk, screaming terribly. I was quite defenceless, for my gun was empty, and my first thought was of escape. I dug my heels into the sides of my horse, but he would not move an inch. The poor animal was paralyzed with terror, and he simply stood still, his fore-legs outstretched, and quivering all over like a leaf.

On rushed the elephant, awful to see; I made one more vain effort to stir the horse. Now the trunk of the great bull swung aloft above my head. A thought flashed through my brain. Quick as light I rolled from the saddle. By the side of the horse lay a fallen tree, as thick through as a man's body. The tree was lifted a little off the ground by the broken boughs which took its weight, and with a single movement, so active is one in such necessities, I flung myself beneath it. As I did so, I heard the trunk of the elephant descend with a mighty thud on the back of my poor horse, and the next instant I was almost in darkness, for the horse, whose back was broken, fell over across the tree under which I lay ensconced. But he did not stop there long. In ten seconds more the bull had wound his trunk about my dead nag's neck, and, with a mighty effort, hurled him clear of the tree. I wriggled backwards as far as I could towards the roots of the tree, for I knew what he was after. Presently I saw the red tip of the bull's trunk stretching itself towards me. If he could manage to hook it round any part of me I was lost. But in the position I occupied, that was just what he could not do, although he knelt down to facilitate his operations. On came the snapping tip like a great open-mouthed snake; it closed upon my hat, which vanished. Again it was thrust down, and a scream of rage was bellowed through it within four inches of my head. Now it seemed to elongate itself. Oh, heavens! now it had me by the hair, which, luckily for myself, was not very long. Then it was my turn to scream, for next instant half a square inch of hair was dragged from my scalp by the roots. I was being plucked alive, as I have seen cruel Kaffir kitchen boys pluck a fowl.

The elephant, however, disappointed with these moderate results, changed his tactics. He wound his trunk round the fallen tree and lifted. The

41

tree stirred, but fortunately the broken branches embedded in the spongy soil, and some roots, which still held, prevented it from being turned over, though he lifted it so much that, had it occurred to him, he could now easily have drawn me out with his trunk. Again he hoisted with all his mighty strength, and I saw that the tree was coming, and roared aloud for help. Some shots were fired close by in answer, but if they hit the bull, their only effect was to stir his energies to more active life. In another few seconds my shelter would be torn away, and I should be done for. A cold perspiration burst out over me as I realized that I was lost. Then of a sudden I remembered that I had a pistol in my belt, which I often used for despatching wounded game. It was loaded and capped. By this time the tree was lifted so much that I could easily get my hand down to my middle and draw the pistol from its case. I drew and cocked it. Now the tree was coming over, and there, within three feet of my head, was the great brown trunk of the elephant. I placed the muzzle of the pistol within an inch of it and fired. The result was instantaneous. Down sunk the tree again, giving one of my legs a considerable squeeze, and next instant I heard a crashing sound. The elephant had bolted.

By this time, what between fright and struggling, I was pretty well tired. I cannot remember how I got from under the fallen tree, or indeed anything, until I found myself sitting on the ground drinking some peach brandy from a flask, and old Indaba-zimbi opposite to me nodding his white lock sagely, while he fired off moral reflections on the narrowness of my escape, and my unwisdom in not having taken his advice to go on foot. That reminded me of my horse--I got up and went to look at it. It was quite dead, the blow of the elephant's trunk had fallen on the saddle, breaking the framework, and rendering it useless. I reflected that in another two seconds it would have fallen on me. Then I called to Indaba-zimbi and asked which way the elephants had gone.

"There!" he said, pointing down the gully, "and we had better go after them, Macumazahn. We have had the bad luck, now for the good."

There was philosophy in this, though, to tell the truth, I did not feel particularly sharp set on elephants at the moment. I seemed to have had enough of them. However, it would never do to show the white feather before the boys, so I assented with much outward readiness, and we started, I on the second horse, and the others on foot. When we had travelled for the best part of an hour down the valley, all of a sudden we came upon the whole herd, which numbered a little more than eighty. Just in front of them the bush was so thick that they seemed to hesitate about entering it, and the sides of the valley were so rocky and steep at this point that they could not climb them.

They saw us at the same moment as we saw them, and inwardly I was filled with fears lest they should take it into their heads to charge back up the gully. But they did not; trumpeting aloud, they rushed at the thick bush which went down before them like corn before a sickle. I do not think that in all my experiences I ever heard anything to equal the sound they made as they crashed through and over the shrubs and trees.

43

Before them was a dense forest belt from a hundred to a hundred and fifty feet in width. As they rushed on, it fell, so that behind them was nothing but a level roadway strewed with fallen trunks, crushed branches, and here and there a tree, too strong even for them, left stranded amid the wreck. On they went, and, notwithstanding the nature of the ground over which they had to travel, they kept their distance ahead of us. This sort of thing continued for a mile or more, and then I saw that in front of the elephants the valley opened into a space covered with reeds and grass--it might have been five or six acres in extent--beyond which the valley ran on again.

The herd reached the edge of this expanse, and for a moment pulled up, hesitating--evidently they mistrusted it. My men yelled aloud, as only Kaffirs can, and that settled them. Headed by the wounded bull, whose martial ardour, like my own, was somewhat cooled, they spread out and dashed into the treacherous swamp--for such it was, though just then there was no water to be seen. For a few yards all went well with them, though they clearly found it heavy going; then suddenly the great bull sank up to his belly in the stiff peaty soil, and remained fixed. The others, mad with fear, took no heed of his struggles and trumpetings, but plunged on to meet the same fate. In five minutes the whole herd of them were hopelessly bogged, and the more they struggled to escape, the deeper they sank. There was one exception, indeed, a cow managed to win back to firm shore, and, lifting her trunk, prepared to charge us as we came up. But at that moment she heard the scream of her calf, and rushed back to its assistance, only to be bogged with the others.

44

Such a scene I never saw before or since. The swamp was spotted all over with the large forms of the elephants, and the air rang with their screams of rage and terror as they waved their trunks wildly to and fro. Now and then a monster would make a great effort and drag his mass from its peaty bed, only to stick fast again at the next step. It was a most pitiable sight, though one that gladdened the hearts of my men. Even the best natives have little compassion for the sufferings of animals.

Well, the rest was easy. The marsh that would not bear the elephants carried our weight well enough. Before midnight all were dead, for we shot them by moonlight. I would gladly have spared the young ones and some of the cows, but to do so would only have meant leaving them to perish of hunger; it was kinder to kill them at once. The wounded bull I slew with my own hand, and I cannot say that I felt much compunction in so doing. He knew me again, and made a desperate effort to get at me, but I am glad to say that the peat held him fast.

The pan presented a curious sight when the sun rose next morning. Owing to the support given by the soil, few of the dead elephants had fallen: there they stood as though they were asleep.

I sent back for the waggons, and when they arrived on the morrow, formed a camp, about a mile away from the pan. Then began the work of cutting out the elephants' tusks; it took over a week, and for obvious reasons was a disgusting task. Indeed, had it not been for the help of some

45

wandering bushmen, who took their pay in elephant meat, I do not think we could ever have managed it.

At last it was done. The ivory was far too cumbersome for us to carry, so we buried it, having first got rid of our bushmen allies. My boys wanted me to go back to the Cape with it and sell it, but I was too much bent on my journey to do this. The tusks lay buried for five years. Then I came and dug them up; they were but little harmed. Ultimately I sold the ivory for something over twelve hundred pounds--not bad pay for one day's shooting.

This was how I began my career as an elephant hunter. I have shot many hundreds of them since, but have never again attempted to do so on horseback.

CHAPTER IV

THE ZULU IMPI

After burying the elephant tusks, and having taken careful notes of the
bearings and peculiarities of the country so that I might be able to
find the spot again, we proceeded on our journey. For a month or more
I trekked along the line which now divides the Orange Free State
from Griqualand West, and the Transvaal from Bechuanaland. The
only difficulties met with were such as are still common to African
travellers--occasional want of water and troubles about crossing sluits
and rivers. I remember that I outspanned on the spot where Kimberley now
stands, and had to press on again in a hurry because there was no water.
I little dreamed then that I should live to see Kimberley a great
city producing millions of pounds worth of diamonds annually, and old
Indaba-zimbi's magic cannot have been worth so much after all, or he
would have told me.

I found the country almost entirely depopulated. Not very long before
Mosilikatze the Lion, Chaka's General had swept across it in his
progress towards what is now Matabeleland. His footsteps were evident
enough. Time upon time I trekked up to what had evidently been the sites
of Kaffir kraals. Now the kraals were ashes and piles of tumbled stones,
and strewn about among the rank grass were the bones of hundreds of men,
women, and children, all of whom had kissed the Zulu assegai. I remember
that in one of these desolate places I found the skull of a child in

47

which a ground-lark had built its nest. It was the twittering of the young birds inside that first called my attention to it. Shortly after this we met with our second great adventure, a much more serious and tragic one than the first.

We were trekking parallel with the Kolong river when a herd of blesbock crossed the track. I fired at one of them and hit it behind. It galloped about a hundred yards with the rest of the herd, then lay down. As we were in want of meat, not having met with any game for a few days past, I jumped on to my horse, and, telling Indaba-zimbi that I would overtake the waggons or meet them on the further side of a rise about an hour's trek away, I started after the wounded buck. As soon as I came within a hundred yards of it, however, it jumped up and ran away as fast

as though it were untouched, only to lie down again at a distance. I followed, thinking that strength would soon fail it. This happened three times. On the third occasion it vanished behind a ridge, and, though by now I was out of both temper and patience, I thought I might as well ride to the crest and see if I could get a shot at it on the further side.

I reached the ridge, which was strewn with stones, looked over it, and saw--a Zulu Impi!

I rubbed my eyes and looked again. Yes, there was no doubt of it. They were halted about a thousand yards away, by the water; some were lying down, some were cooking at fires, others were stalking about with spears and shields in their hands; there might have been two thousand or more of them in all. While I was wondering--and that with no little uneasiness--what on earth they could be doing there, suddenly I heard a wild cry to the right and left of me. I glanced first one way, then the other. From either side a great Zulu was bearing down on me, their broad stabbing assegais aloft, and black shields in their left hands. The man to the right was about fifteen yards away, he to the left was not more than ten. On they came, their fierce eyes almost starting out of their heads, and I felt, with a cold thrill of fear, that in another three seconds those broad "bangwans" might be buried in my vitals. On such occasions we act, I suppose, more from instinct than from anything else--there is no time for thought. At any rate, I dropped the reins and, raising my gun, fired point blank at the left-hand man. The bullet struck him in the middle of his shield, pierced it, and passed through him, and over he rolled upon the veldt. I swung round in the saddle; most happily my horse was accustomed to standing still when I fired from his back, also he was so surprised that he did not know which way to shy. The other savage was almost on me; his outstretched shield reached the muzzle of my gun as I pulled the trigger of the left barrel. It exploded, the warrior sprung high into the air, and fell against my horse dead, his spear passing just in front of my face.

Without waiting to reload, or even to look if the main body of the Zulus had seen the death of their two scouts, I turned my horse and drove my heels into his sides. As soon as I was down the slope of the rise I pulled a little to the right in order to intercept the waggons before the Zulus saw them. I had not gone three hundred yards in this new direction when, to my utter astonishment, I struck a trail marked with waggon-wheels and the hoofs of oxen. Of waggons there must have been at least eight, and several hundred cattle. Moreover, they had passed within twelve hours; I could tell that by the spoor. Then I understood; the Impi was following the track of the waggons, which, in all probability, belonged to a party of emigrant Boers.

The spoor of the waggons ran in the direction I wished to go, so I followed it. About a mile further on I came to the crest of a rise, and there, about five furlongs away, I saw the waggons drawn up in a rough laager upon the banks of the river. There, too, were my own waggons trekking down the slope towards them.

In another five minutes I was there. The Boers--for Boers they were--were standing about outside the little laager watching the approach of my two waggons. I called to them, and they turned and saw me. The very first man my eyes fell on was a Boer named Hans Botha, whom I had known well years ago in the Cape. He was not a bad specimen of his class, but a very restless person, with a great objection to authority, or, as he expressed it, "a love of freedom." He had joined a party of the emigrant Boers some years before, but, as I learned presently, had quarrelled with its leader, and was now trekking away into the wilderness to found a little colony of his own. Poor fellow! It was his last trek.

"How do you do, Meinheer Botha?" I said to him in Dutch.

The man looked at me, looked again, then, startled out of his Dutch stolidity, cried to his wife, who was seated on the box of the waggon--

"Come here, Frau, come. Here is Allan Quatermain, the Englishman, the son of the 'Predicant.' How goes it, Heer Quatermain, and what is the news down in the Cape yonder?"

"I don't know what the news is in the Cape, Hans," I answered, solemnly; "but the news here is that there is a Zulu Impi upon your spoor and within two miles of the waggons. That I know, for I have just shot two of their sentries," and I showed him my empty gun.

For a moment there was a silence of astonishment, and I saw the bronzed faces of the men turn pale beneath their tan, while one or two of the women gave a little scream, and the children crept to their sides.

"Almighty!" cried Hans, "that must be the Umtetwa Regiment that Dingaan sent against the Basutus, but who could not come at them because of the marshes, and so were afraid to return to Zululand, and struck north to join Mosilikatze."

"Laager up, Carles! Laager up for your lives, and one of you jump on a horse and drive in the cattle."

51

At this moment my own waggons came up. Indaba-zimbi was sitting on the box of the first, wrapped in a blanket. I called him and told him the news.

"Ill tidings, Macumazahn," he said; "there will be dead Boers about to-morrow morning, but they will not attack till dawn, then they will wipe out the laager so!" and he passed his hand before his mouth.

"Stop that croaking, you white-headed crow," I said, though I knew his words were true. What chance had a laager of ten waggons all told against at least two thousand of the bravest savages in the world?

"Macumazahn, will you take my advice this time?" Indaba-zimbi said, presently.

"What is it?" I asked.

"This. Leave your waggons here, jump on that horse, and let us two run for it as hard as we can go. The Zulus won't follow us, they will be looking after the Boers."

"I won't leave the other white men," I said; "it would be the act of a coward. If I die, I die."

"Very well, Macumazahn, then stay and be killed," he answered, taking a pinch of snuff. "Come, let us see about the waggons," and we walked towards the laager.

Here everything was in confusion. However, I got hold of Hans Botha and put it to him if it would not be best to desert the waggons and make a run for it.

"How can we do it?" he answered; "two of the women are too fat to go a mile, one is sick in childbed, and we have only six horses among us. Besides, if we did we should starve in the desert. No, Heer Allan, we must fight it out with the savages, and God help us!"

"God help us, indeed. Think of the children, Hans!"

"I can't bear to think," he answered, in a broken voice, looking at his own little girl, a sweet, curly-haired, blue-eyed child of six, named Tota, whom I had often nursed as a baby. "Oh, Heer Allan, your father, the Predicant, always warned me against trekking north, and I never would listen to him because I thought him a cursed Englishman; now I see my folly. Heer Allan, if you can, try to save my child from those black devils; if you live longer than I do, or if you can't save her, kill her," and he clasped my hand.

"It hasn't come to that yet, Hans," I said.

Then we set to work on the laager. The waggons, of which, including

53

my two, there were ten, were drawn into the form of a square, and the disselboom of each securely lashed with reims to the underworks of that in front of it. The wheels also were locked, and the space between the ground and the bed-planks of the waggons was stuffed with branches of the "wait-a-bit" thorn that fortunately grew near in considerable quantities. In this way a barrier was formed of no mean strength as against a foe unprovided with firearms, places being left for the men to fire from. In a little over an hour everything was done that could be done, and a discussion arose as to the disposal of the cattle, which had been driven up close to the camp. Some of the Boers were anxious to get them into the laager, small as it was, or at least as many of them as it would hold. I argued strongly against this, pointing out that the brutes would probably be seized with panic as soon as the firing began, and trample the defenders of the laager under foot. As an alternative plan I suggested that some of the native servants should drive the herd along the valley of the river till they reached a friendly tribe or some other place of safety. Of course, if the Zulus saw them they would be taken, but the nature of the ground was favourable, and it was possible that they might escape if they started at once. The proposition was promptly agreed to, and, what is more, it was settled that one Dutchman and such of the women and children as could travel should go with them. In half an hour's time twelve of them started with the natives, the Boer in charge, and the cattle. Three of my own men went with the latter, the three others and Indaba-zimbi stopped with me in the laager.

The parting was a heart-breaking scene, upon which I do not care to dwell. The women wept, the men groaned, and the children looked on with scared white faces. At length they were gone, and I for one was thankful of it. There remained in the laager seventeen white men, four natives, the two Boer fraus who were too stout to travel, the woman in childbed and her baby, and Hans Bother's little daughter Tota, whom he could not make up his mind to part with. Happily her mother was already dead. And here I may state that ten of the women and children, together with about half of the cattle, escaped. The Zulu Impi never saw them, and on the third day of travel they came to the fortified place of a Griqua chief, who sheltered them on receiving half the cattle in payment. Thence by slow degrees they journeyed down to the Cape Colony, reaching a civilized region within a little more than a year from the date of the attack on the laager.

The afternoon was now drawing towards evening, but still there were no signs of the Impi. A wild hope struck us that they might have gone on about their business. Ever since Indaba-zimbi had heard that the regiment was supposed to belong to the Umtetwa tribe, he had, I noticed, been plunged in deep thought. Presently he came to me and volunteered to go out and spy upon their movements. At first Hans Botha was against this idea, saying that he was a "verdomde swartzel"--an accursed black creature--and would betray us. I pointed out that there was nothing to betray. The Zulus must know where the waggons were, but it was important for us to gain information of their movements. So it was agreed that Indaba-zimbi should go. I told him this. He nodded his white lock, said "All right, Macumazahn," and started. I noticed with some surprise, however, that before he did so he went to the waggon and fetched his "mouti," or medicine, which, together with his other magical apparatus, he always carried in a skin bag. I asked him why he did this. He answered that it was to make himself invulnerable against the spears of the Zulus. I did not in the least believe his explanation, for in my heart I was sure that he meant to take the opportunity to make a bolt of it, leaving me to my fate. I did not, however, interfere to prevent this, for I had an affection for the old fellow, and sincerely hoped that he might escape the doom which overshadowed us.

So Indaba-zimbi sauntered off, and as I looked at his retreating form I thought I should never see it again. But I was mistaken, and little knew that he was risking his life, not for the Boers whom he hated one and all, but for me whom in his queer way he loved.

When he had gone we completed our preparations for defence, strengthening the waggons and the thorns beneath with earth and stones. Then at sunset we ate and drank as heartily as we could under the circumstances, and when we had done, Hans Botha, as head of the party, offered up prayer to God for our preservation. It was a touching sight to see the burly Dutchman, his hat off, his broad face lit up by the last rays of the setting sun, praying aloud in homely, simple language to Him who alone could save us from the spears of a cruel foe. I remember that the last sentence of his prayer was, "Almighty, if we must be killed, save the women and children and my little girl Tota from the accursed Zulus, and do not let us be tortured."

I echoed the request very earnestly in my own heart, that I know, for in common with the others I was dreadfully afraid, and it must be admitted not without reason.

Then the darkness came on, and we took up our appointed places each with a rifle in his hands and peered out into the gloom in silence. Occasionally one of the Boers would light his pipe with a brand from the smouldering fire, and the glow of it would shine for a few moments on his pale, anxious face.

Behind me one of the stout "fraus" lay upon the ground. Even the terror of our position could not keep her heavy eyes from their accustomed sleep, and she snored loudly. On the further side of her, just by the fire, lay little Tota, wrapped in a kaross. She was asleep also, her thumb in her mouth, and from time to time her father would come to look at her.

So the hours wore on while we waited for the Zulus. But from my intimate knowledge of the habits of natives I had little fear that they would attack us at night, though, had they done so, they could have compassed our destruction with but small loss to themselves. It is not the habit of this people, they like to fight in the light of day--at dawn for preference.

About eleven o'clock, just as I was nodding a little at my post, I heard a low whistle outside the laager. Instantly I was wide awake, and all along the line I heard the clicking of locks as the Boers cocked their guns.

"Macumazahn," said a voice, the voice of Indaba-zimbi, "are you there?"

"Yes," I answered.

"Then hold a light so that I can see how to climb into the laager," he said.

"Yah! yah! hold a light," put in one of the Boers. "I don't trust that black schepsel of yours, Heer Quatermain; he may have some of his countrymen with him." Accordingly a lantern was produced and held towards the voice. There was Indaba-zimbi alone. We let him into the laager and asked him the news.

"This is the news, white men," he said. "I waited till dark, and creeping up to the place where the Zulus are encamped, hid myself behind a stone and listened. They are a great regiment of Umtetwas as Baas Botha yonder thought. They struck the spoor of the waggons three days ago and followed it. To-night they sleep upon their spears, to-morrow at daybreak they will attack the laager and kill everybody. They are very bitter against the Boers, because of the battle at Blood River and the other fights, and that is why they followed the waggons instead of going straight north after Mosilikatze."

58

A kind of groan went up from the group of listening Dutchmen.

"I tell you what it is, Heeren," I said, "instead of waiting to be butchered here like buck in a pitfall, let us go out now and fall upon the Impi while it sleeps."

This proposition excited some discussion, but in the end only one man could be found to vote for it. Boers as a rule lack that dash which makes great soldiers; such forlorn hopes are not in their line, and rather than embark upon them they prefer to take their chance in a laager, however poor that chance may be. For my own part I firmly believe that had my advice been taken we should have routed the Zulus. Seventeen desperate white men, armed with guns, would have produced no small effect upon a camp of sleeping savages. But it was not taken, so it is no use talking about it.

After that we went back to our posts, and slowly the weary night wore on towards the dawn. Only those who have watched under similar circumstances while they waited the advent of almost certain and cruel death, can know the torturing suspense of those heavy hours. But they went somehow, and at last in the far east the sky began to lighten, while the cold breath of dawn stirred the tilts of the waggons and chilled me to the bone. The fat Dutchwoman behind me woke with a yawn, then, remembering all, moaned aloud, while her teeth chattered with cold and fear. Hans Botha went to his waggon and got a bottle of peach brandy, from which he poured into a tin pannikin, giving us each a stiff dram, and making attempts to be cheerful as he did so. But his affected jocularity only seemed to depress his comrades the more. Certainly it depressed me.

Now the light was growing, and we could see some way into the mist which still hung densely over the river, and now--ah! there it was. From the other side of the hill, a thousand yards or more from the laager, came a faint humming sound. It grew and grew till it gathered to a chant--the awful war chant of the Zulus. Soon I could catch the words. They were simple enough:

"We shall slay, we shall slay! Is it not so, my brothers? Our spears shall blush blood-red. Is it not so, my brothers? For we are the sucklings of Chaka, blood is our milk, my brothers. Awake, children of the Umtetwa, awake! The vulture wheels, the jackal sniffs the air; Awake, children of the Umtetwa--cry aloud, ye ringed men: There is the foe, we shall slay them. Is it not so, my brothers? S'gee! S'gee! S'gee!"

Such is a rough translation of that hateful chant which to this very day I often seem to hear. It does not look particularly imposing on paper, but if, while he waited to be killed, the reader could have heard it as it rolled through the still air from the throats of nearly three thousand warriors singing all to time, he would have found it impressive enough.

Now the shields began to appear over the brow of the rise. They came
by companies, each company about ninety strong. Altogether there were
thirty-one companies. I counted them. When all were over they formed
themselves into a triple line, then trotted down the slope towards us.
At a distance of a hundred and fifty yards or just out of the shot of
such guns as we had in those days, they halted and began singing again--

"Yonder is the kraal of the white man--a little kraal, my
brothers;
We shall eat it up, we shall trample it flat, my brothers.
But where are the white man's cattle--where are his oxen, my
brothers?"

This question seemed to puzzle them a good deal, for they sang the song
again and again. At last a herald came forward, a great man with ivory
rings about his arm, and, putting his hands to his mouth, called out to
us asking where our cattle were.

Hans Botha climbed on to the top of a waggon and roared out that they
might answer that question themselves.

Then the herald called again, saying that he saw the cattle had been
sent away.

"We shall go and find the cattle," he said, "then we shall come and kill you, because without cattle you must stop where you are, but if we wait to kill you before we get the cattle, they may have trekked too far for us to follow. And if you try to run away we shall easily catch you white men!"

This struck me as a very odd speech, for the Zulus generally attack an enemy first and take his cattle afterwards; still, there was a certain amount of plausibility about it. While I was still wondering what it all might mean, the Zulus began to run past us in companies towards the river. Suddenly a shout announced that they had found the spoor of the cattle, and the whole Impi of them started down it at a run till they vanished over a rise about a quarter of a mile away.

We waited for half an hour or more, but nothing could we see of them.

"Now I wonder if the devils have really gone," said Hans Botha to me. "It is very strange."

"I will go and see," said Indaba-zimbi, "if you will come with me, Macumazahn. We can creep to the top of the ridge and look over."

At first I hesitated, but curiosity overcame me. I was young in those days and weary with suspense.

"Very well," I said, "we will go."

So we started. I had my elephant gun and ammunition. Indaba-zimbi had his medicine bag and an assegai. We crept to the top of the rise like sportsmen stalking a buck. The slope on the other side was strewn with rocks, among which grew bushes and tall grass.

"They must have gone down the Donga," I said to Indaba-zimbi, "I can't see one of them."

As I spoke there came a roar of men all round me. From every rock, from every tuft of grass rose a Zulu warrior. Before I could turn, before I could lift a gun, I was seized and thrown.

"Hold him! Hold the White Spirit fast!" cried a voice. "Hold him, or he will slip away like a snake. Don't hurt him, but hold him fast. Let Indaba-zimbi walk by his side."

I turned on Indaba-zimbi. "You black devil, you have betrayed me!" I cried.

"Wait and see, Macumazahn," he answered, coolly. "Now the fight is going to begin."

CHAPTER V

THE END OF THE LAAGER

I gasped with wonder and rage. What did that scoundrel Indaba-zimbi mean? Why had I been drawn out of the laager and seized, and why, being seized, was I not instantly killed? They called me the "White Spirit." Could it be that they were keeping me to make me into medicine? I had heard of such things being done by Zulus and kindred tribes, and my blood ran cold at the thought. What an end! To be pounded up, made medicine of, and eaten!

However, I had little time for further reflection, for now the whole Impi was pouring back from the donga and river-banks where it had hidden while their ruse was carried out, and once more formed up on the side of the slope. I was taken to the crest of the slope and placed in the centre of the reserve line in the especial charge of a huge Zulu named Bombyane, the same man who had come forward as a herald. This brute seemed to regard me with an affectionate curiosity. Now and again he poked me in the ribs with the handle of his assegai, as though to assure himself that I was solid, and several times he asked me to be so good as to prophesy how many Zulus would be killed before the "Amaboona," as they called the Boers, were "eaten up."

At first I took no notice of him beyond scowling, but presently, goaded into anger, I prophesied that he would be dead in an hour!

He only laughed aloud. "Oh! White Spirit," he said, "is it so? Well, I've walked a long way from Zululand, and shall be glad of a rest."

And he got it shortly, as will be seen.

Now the Zulus began to sing again--

"We have caught the White Spirit, my brother! my brother!
Iron-Tongue whispered of him, he smelt him out, my brother.
Now the Maboona are ours--they are already dead, my brother."

So that treacherous villain Indaba-zimbi had betrayed me. Suddenly the chief of the Impi, a grey-haired man named Sususa, held up his assegai, and instantly there was silence. Then he spoke to some indunas who stood near him. Instantly they ran to the right and left down the first line, saying a word to the captain of each company as they passed him. Presently they were at the respective ends of the line, and simultaneously held up their spears. As they did so, with an awful roar of "Bulala Amaboona"--"Slay the Boers," the entire line, numbering nearly a thousand men, bounded forward like a buck startled from its form, and rushed down upon the little laager. It was a splendid sight to see them, their assegais glittering in the sunlight as they rose and fell above their black shields, their war-plumes bending back upon the wind, and their fierce faces set intently on the foe, while the solid earth shook beneath the thunder of their rushing feet. I thought of my poor friends the Dutchmen, and trembled. What chance had they against so many?

Now the Zulus, running in the shape of a bow so as to wrap the laager round on three sides, were within seventy yards, and now from every waggon broke tongues of fire. Over rolled a number of the Umtetwa, but the rest cared little. Forward they sped straight to the laager, striving to force a way in. But the Boers plied them with volley after volley, and, packed as the Zulus were, the elephant guns loaded with slugs and small shot did frightful execution. Only one man even got on to a waggon, and as he did so I saw a Boer woman strike him on the head with an axe. He fell down, and slowly, amid howls of derision from the two lines on the hill-side, the Zulus drew back.

"Let us go, father!" shouted the soldiers on the slope, among whom I was, to their chief, who had come up. "You have sent out the little girls to fight, and they are frightened. Let us show them the way."

"No, no!" the chief Sususa answered, laughing. "Wait a minute and the little girls will grow to women, and women are good enough to fight against Boers!"

The attacking Zulus heard the mockery of their fellows, and rushed forward again with a roar. But the Boers in the laager had found time to load, and they met with a warm reception. Reserving their fire till the Zulus were packed like sheep in a kraal, they loosed into them with the

roers, and the warriors fell in little heaps. But I saw that the blood
of the Umtetwas was up; they did not mean to be beaten back this time,
and the end was near. See! six men had leapt on to a waggon, slain the
man behind it, and sprung into the laager. They were killed there, but
others followed, and then I turned my head. But I could not shut my ears
to the cries of rage and death, and the terrible S'gee! S'gee! of the
savages as they did their work of murder. Once only I looked up and saw
poor Hans Botha standing on a waggon smiting down men with the butt of
his rifle. The assegais shot up towards him like tongues of steel, and
when I looked again he was gone.

I turned sick with fear and rage. But alas! what could I do? They were
all dead now, and probably my own turn was coming, only my death with
not be so swift.

The fight was ended, and the two lines on the slope broke their order,
and moved down to the laager. Presently we were there, and a dreadful
sight it was. Many of the attacking Zulus were dead--quite fifty I
should say, and at least a hundred and fifty were wounded, some of them
mortally. The chief Sususa gave an order, the dead men were picked up
and piled in a heap, while those who were slightly hurt walked off to
find some one to tie up their wounds. But the more serious cases met
with a different treatment. The chief or one of his indunas considered
each case, and if it was in any way bad, the man was taken up and thrown
into the river which ran near. None of them offered any objection,
though one poor fellow swam to shore again. He did not stop there long,

however, for they pushed him back and drowned him by force.

The strangest case of all was that of the chief's own brother. He had been captain of the line, and his ankle was smashed by a bullet. Sususa came up to him, and, having examined the wound, rated him soundly for failing in the first onslaught.

The poor fellow made the excuse that it was not his fault, as the Boers had hit him in the first rush. His brother admitted the truth of this, and talked to him amicably.

"Well," he said at length, offering him a pinch of snuff, "you cannot walk again."

"No, chief," said the wounded man, looking at his ankle.

"And to-morrow we must walk far," went on Sususa.

"Yes, chief."

"Say, then, will you sit here on the veldt, or----" and he nodded towards the river.

The man dropped his head on his breast for a minute as though in thought. Presently he lifted it and looked Sususa straight in the face.

"My ankle pains me, my brother," he said; "I think I will go back to Zululand, for there is the only kraal I wish to see again, even if I creep about it like a snake."[*]

[*] The Zulus believe that after death their spirits enter into the bodies of large green snakes, which glide about the kraals. To kill these snakes is sacrilege.

"It is well, my brother," said the chief. "Rest softly," and having shaken hands with him, he gave an order to one of the indunas, and turned away.

Then men came, and, supporting the wounded man, led him down to the banks of the stream. Here, at his request, they tied a heavy stone round his neck, and then threw him into a deep pool. I saw the whole sad scene, and the victim never even winced. It was impossible not to admire the extraordinary courage of the man, or to avoid being struck with the cold-blooded cruelty of his brother the chief. And yet the act was necessary from his point of view. The man must either die swiftly, or be left to perish of starvation, for no Zulu force will encumber itself with wounded men. Years of merciless warfare had so hardened these people that they looked on death as nothing, and were, to do them justice, as willing to meet it themselves as to inflict it on others. When this very Impi had been sent out by the Zulu King Dingaan, it consisted of some nine thousand men. Now it numbered less than three; all the rest were dead. They, too, would probably soon be dead. What did

69

it matter? They lived by war to die in blood. It was their natural end. "Kill till you are killed." That is the motto of the Zulu soldier. It has the merit of simplicity.

Meanwhile the warriors were looting the waggons, including my own, having first thrown all the dead Boers into a heap. I looked at the heap; all of them were there, including the two stout fraus, poor things. But I missed one body, that of Hans Botha's daughter, little Tota. A wild hope came into my heart that she might have escaped; but no, it was not possible. I could only pray that she was already at rest.

Just then the great Zulu, Bombyane, who had left my side to indulge in the congenial occupation of looting, came out of a waggon crying that he had got the "little white one." I looked; he was carrying the child Tota, gripping her frock in one of his huge black hands. He stalked up to where we were, and held the child before the chief. "Is it dead, father?" he said, with a laugh.

Now, as I could well see, the child was not dead, but had been hidden away, and fainted with fear.

The chief glanced at it carelessly, and said--

"Find out with your kerrie."

Acting on this hint the black devil held up the child, and was about to kill it with his knobstick. This was more than I could bear. I sprang at him and struck him with all my force in the face, little caring if I was speared or not. He dropped Tota on the ground.

"Ou!" he said, putting his hand to his nose, "the White Spirit has a hard fist. Come, Spirit, I will fight you for the child."

The soldiers cheered and laughed. "Yes! yes!" they said, "let Bombyane fight the White Spirit for the child. Let them fight with assegais."

For a moment I hesitated. What chance had I against this black giant? But I had promised poor Hans to save the child if I could, and what did it matter? As well die now as later. However, I had wit enough left to make a favour of it, and intimated to the chief through Indaba-zimbi that I was quite willing to condescend to kill Bombyane, on condition that if I did so the child's life should be given to me. Indaba-zimbi interpreted my words, but I noticed that he would not look on me as he spoke, but covered his face with his hands and spoke of me as "the ghost" or the "son of the spirit." For some reason that I have never quite understood, the chief consented to the duel. I fancy it was because he believed me to be more than mortal, and was anxious to see the last of Bombyane.

"Let them fight," he said. "Give them assegais and no shields; the child shall be to him who conquers."

"Yes! yes!" cried the soldiers. "Let them fight. Don't be afraid, Bombyane; if he is a spirit, he's a very small one."

"I never was frightened of man or beast, and I am not going to run away from a White Ghost," answered the redoubtable Bombyane, as he examined the blade of his great bangwan or stabbing assegai.

Then they made a ring round us, gave me a similar assegai, and set us some ten paces apart. I kept my face as calm as I could, and tried to show no signs of fear, though in my heart I was terribly afraid. Humanly speaking, my doom was on me. The giant warrior before me had used the assegai from a child--I had no experience of the weapon. Moreover, though I was quick and active, he must have been at least twice as strong as I am. However, there was no help for it, so, setting my teeth, I grasped the great spear, breathed a prayer, and waited.

The giant stood awhile looking at me, and, as he stood, Indaba-zimbi walked across the ring behind me, muttering as he passed, "Keep cool, Macumazahn, and wait for him. I will make it all right."

As I had not the slightest intention of commencing the fray, I thought this good advice, though how Indaba-zimbi could "make it all right" I failed to see.

Heavens! how long that half-minute seemed! It happened many years ago, but the whole scene rises up before my eyes as I write. There behind us was the blood-stained laager, and near it lay the piles of dead; round us was rank upon rank of plumed savages, standing in silence to wait the issue of the duel, and in the centre stood the grey-haired chief and general, Sususa, in all his war finery, a cloak of leopard skin upon his shoulders. At his feet lay the senseless form of little Tota, to my left squatted Indaba-zimbi, nodding his white lock and muttering something--probably spells; while in front was my giant antagonist, his spear aloft and his plumes wavering in the gentle wind. Then over all, over grassy slope, river, and koppie, over the waggons of the laager, the piles of dead, the dense masses of the living, the swooning child, over all shone the bright impartial sun, looking down like the indifferent eye of Heaven upon the loveliness of nature and the cruelty of man. Down by the river grew thorn-trees, and from them floated the sweet scent of the mimosa flower, and came the sound of cooing turtle-doves. I never smell the one or hear the other without the scene flashing into my mind again, complete in its every detail.

Suddenly, without a sound, Bombyane shook his assegai and rushed straight at me. I saw his huge form come; like a man in a dream, I saw the broad spear flash on high; now he was on me! Then, prompted to it by some providential impulse--or had the spells of Indaba-zimbi anything to do with the matter?--I dropped to my knee, and quick as light stretched out my spear. He drove at me: the blade passed over my head. I felt a weight on my assegai; it was wrenched from my hand; his great limbs knocked against me. I glanced round. Bombyane was staggering along with head thrown back and outstretched arms from which his spear had fallen.

His spear had fallen, but the blade of mine stood out between his shoulders--I had transfixed him. He stopped, swung slowly round as though to look at me: then with a sigh the giant sank down--dead.

For a moment there was silence; then a great cry rose--a cry of "Bombyane is dead. The White Spirit has slain Bombyane. Kill the wizard, kill the ghost who has slain Bombyane by witchcraft."

Instantly I was surrounded by fierce faces, and spears flashed before my eyes. I folded my arms and stood calmly waiting the end. In a moment it would have come, for the warriors were mad at seeing their champion overthrown thus easily. But presently through the tumult I heard the high, cracked voice of Indaba-zimbi.

"Stand back, you fools!" it cried; "can a spirit then be killed?"

"Spear him! spear him!" they roared in fury. "Let us see if he is a spirit. How did a spirit slay Bombyane with an assegai? Spear him, rain-maker, and we shall see."

"Stand back," cried Indaba-zimbi again, "and I will show you if he can be killed. I will kill him myself, and call him back to life again before your eyes."

"Macumazahn, trust me," he whispered in my ear in the Sisutu tongue, which the Zulus did not understand. "Trust me; kneel on the grass before

74

me, and when I strike at you with the spear, roll over like one dead; then, when you hear my voice again, get up. Trust me--it is your only hope."

Having no choice I nodded my head in assent, though I had not the faintest idea of what he was about to do. The tumult lessened somewhat, and once more the warriors drew back.

"Great White Spirit--Spirit of victory," said Indaba-zimbi, addressing me aloud, and covering his eyes with his hand, "hear me and forgive me. These children are blind with folly, and think thee mortal because thou hast dealt death upon a mortal who dared to stand against thee. Deign to kneel down before me and let me pierce thy heart with this spear, then when I call upon thee, arise unhurt."

I knelt down, not because I wished to, but because I must. I had not overmuch faith in Indaba-zimbi, and thought it probable that he was in truth about to make an end of me. But really I was so worn out with fears, and the horrors of the night and day had so shaken my nerves, that I did not greatly care what befell me. When I had been kneeling thus for about half a minute Indaba-zimbi spoke.

"People of the Umtetwa, children of T'Chaka," he said, "draw back a little way, lest an evil fall on you, for now the air is thick with ghosts."

They drew back a space, leaving us in a circle about twelve yards in diameter.

"Look on him who kneels before you," went on Indaba-zimbi, "and listen to my words, to the words of the witch-finder, the words of the rain-maker, Indaba-zimbi, whose fame is known to you. He seems to be a young man, does he not? I tell you, children of the Umtetwa, he is no man. He is the Spirit who gives victory to the white men, he it is who gave them assegais that thunder and taught them how to slay. Why were the Impis of Dingaan rolled back at the Blood River? Because he was there. Why did the Amaboona slay the people of Mosilikatze by the thousand? Because he was there. And so I say to you that, had I not drawn him from the laager by my magic but three hours ago, you would have been conquered--yes, you would have been blown away like the dust before the wind; you would have been burnt up like the dry grass in the winter when the fire is awake among it. Ay, because he had but been there many of your bravest were slain in overcoming a few--a pinch of men who could be counted on the fingers. But because I loved you, because your chief Sususa is my half-brother--for had we not one father?--I came to you, I warned you. Then you prayed me and I drew the Spirit forth. But you were not satisfied when the victory was yours, when the Spirit, of all you had taken asked but one little thing--a white child to take away and sacrifice to himself, to make the medicine of his magic of----"

Here I could hardly restrain myself from interrupting, but thought better of it.

"You said him nay; you said, 'Let him fight with our bravest man, let him fight with Bombyane the giant for the child.' And he deigned to slay Bombyane as you have seen, and now you say, 'Slay him; he is no spirit.' Now I will show you if he is a spirit, for I will slay him before your eyes, and call him to life again. But you have brought this upon yourselves. Had you believed, had you offered no insult to the Spirit, he would have stayed with you, and you should have become unconquerable. Now he will arise and leave you, and woe be on you if you try to stay him.

"Now all men," he went on, "look for a space upon this assegai that I hold up," and he lifted the bangwan of the deceased Bombyane high above his head so that all the multitude could see it. Every eye was fixed upon the broad bright spear. For a while he held it still, then he moved it round and round in a circle, muttering as he did so, and still their gaze followed it. For my part, I watched his movements with the greatest anxiety. That assegai had already been nearer my person than I found at all pleasant, and I had no desire to make a further acquaintance with it. Nor, indeed, was I sure that Indaba-zimbi was not really going to kill me. I could not understand his proceedings at all, and at the best I did not relish playing the corpus vile to his magical experiments.

"Look! look! look!" he screamed.

Then suddenly the great spear flashed down towards my breast. I felt nothing, but, to my sight, it seemed as though it had passed through me.

"See!" roared the Zulus. "Indaba-zimbi has speared him; the red assegai stands out behind his back."

"Roll over, Macumazahn," Indaba-zimbi hissed in my ear, "roll over and pretend to die--quick! quick!"

I lost no time in following these strange instructions, but falling on to my side, threw my arms wide, kicked my legs about, and died as artistically as I could. Presently I gave a stage shiver and lay still.

"See!" said the Zulus, "he is dead, the Spirit is dead. Look at the blood upon the assegai!"

"Stand back! stand back!" cried Indaba-zimbi, "or the ghost will haunt you. Yes, he is dead, and now I will call him back to life again. Look!" and putting down his hand, he plucked the spear from wherever it was fixed, and held it aloft. "The spear is red, is it not? Watch, men, watch! it grows white!"

"Yes, it grows white," they said. "Ou! it grows white."

"It grows white because the blood returns to whence it came," said Indaba-zimbi. "Now, great Spirit, hear me. Thou art dead, the breath has

78

gone out of thy mouth. Yet hear me and arise. Awake, White Spirit, awake and show thy power. Awake! arise unhurt!"

I began to respond cheerfully to this imposing invocation.

"Not so fast, Macumazahn," whispered Indaba-zimbi.

I took the hint, and first held up my arm, then lifted my head and let it fall again.

"He lives! by the head of T'Chaka he lives!" roared the soldiers, stricken with mortal fear.

Then slowly and with the greatest dignity I gradually arose, stretched my arms, yawned like one awaking from heavy sleep, turned and looked upon them unconcernedly. While I did so, I noticed that old Indaba-zimbi was almost fainting from exhaustion. Beads of perspiration stood upon his brow, his limbs trembled, and his breast heaved.

As for the Zulus, they waited for no more. With a howl of terror the whole regiment turned and fled across the rise, so that presently we were left alone with the dead, and the swooning child.

"How on earth did you do that, Indaba-zimbi?" I asked in amaze.

"Do not ask me, Macumazahn," he gasped. "You white men are very clever, but you don't quite know everything. There are men in the world who can make people believe they see things which they do not see. Let us be going while we may, for when those Umtetwas have got over their fright, they will come back to loot the waggons, and then perhaps they will begin asking questions that I can't answer."

And here I may as well state that I never got any further information on this matter from old Indaba-zimbi. But I have my theory, and here it is for whatever it may be worth. I believe that Indaba-zimbi mesmerized the whole crowd of onlookers, myself included, making them believe that they saw the assegai in my heart, and the blood upon the blade. The reader may smile and say, "Impossible;" but I would ask him how the Indian jugglers do their tricks unless it is by mesmerism. The spectators seem to see the boy go under the basket and there pierced with daggers, they seem to see women in a trance supported in mid-air upon the point of a single sword. In themselves these things are not possible, they violate the laws of nature, as those laws are known to us, and therefore must surely be illusion. And so through the glamour thrown upon them by Indaba-zimbi's will, that Zulu Impi seemed to see me transfixed with an assegai which never touched me. At least, that is my theory; if any one has a better, let him adopt it. The explanation lies between illusion and magic of a most imposing character, and I prefer to accept the first alternative.

CHAPTER VI

STELLA

I was not slow to take Indaba-zimbi's hint. About a hundred and fifty yards to the left of the laager was a little dell where I had hidden my horse, together with one belonging to the Boers, and my saddle and bridle. Thither we went, I carrying the swooning Tota in my arms. To our joy we found the horses safe, for the Zulus had not seen them. Now, of course, they were our only means of locomotion, for the oxen had been sent away, and even had they been there we could not have found time to inspan them. I laid Tota down, caught my horse, undid his knee halter, and saddled up. As I was doing so a thought struck me, and I told Indaba-zimbi to run to the laager and see if he could find my double-barrelled gun and some powder and shot, for I had only my elephant "roer" and a few charges of powder and ball with me.

He went, and while he was away, poor little Tota came to herself and began to cry, till she saw my face.

"Ah, I have had such a bad dream," she said, in Dutch: "I dreamed that the black Kaffirs were going to kill me. Where is my papa?"

I winced at the question. "Your papa has gone on a journey, dear," I said, "and left me to look after you. We shall find him one day. You don't mind going with Heer Allan, do you?"

81

"No," she said, a little doubtfully, and began to cry again. Presently she remembered that she was thirsty, and asked for water. I led her to the river and she drank. "Why is my hand red, Heer Allan?" she asked, pointing to the smear of Bombyane's blood-stained fingers.

At this moment I felt very glad that I had killed Bombyane.

"It is only paint, dear," I said; "see, we will wash it and your face."

As I was doing this, Indaba-zimbi returned. The guns were all gone; he said the Zulus had taken them and the powder. But he had found some things and brought them in a sack. There was a thick blanket, about twenty pounds weight of biltong or sun-dried meat, a few double-handfuls of biscuits, two water-bottles, a tin pannikin, some matches and sundries.

"And now, Macumazahn," he said, "we had best be going, for those Umtetwas are coming back. I saw one of them on the brow of the rise."

That was enough for me. I lifted little Tota on to the bow of my saddle, climbed into it, and rode off, holding her in front of me. Indaba-zimbi slipped a reim into the mouth of the best of the Boer horses, threw of the sack of sundries on to its back and mounted also, holding the elephant gun in his hand. We went eight or nine hundred yards in silence till we were quite out of range of sight from the waggons, which were in a hollow. Then I pulled up, with such a feeling of thankfulness in my heart as cannot be told in words; for now I knew that, mounted as we were, those black demons could never catch us. But where were we to steer for? I put the question to Indaba-zimbi, asking him if he thought that we had better try and follow the oxen which we had sent away with the Kaffirs and women on the preceding night. He shook his head.

"The Umtetwas will go after the oxen presently," he answered, "and we have seen enough of them."

"Quite enough," I answered, with enthusiasm; "I never want to see another; but where are we to go? Here we are alone with one gun and a little girl in the vast and lonely veldt. Which way shall we turn?"

"Our faces were towards the north before we met the Zulus," answered Indaba-zimbi; "let us still keep them to the north. Ride on, Macumazahn; to-night when we off-saddle I will look into the matter."

So all that long afternoon we rode on, following the course of the river. From the nature of the ground we could only go slowly, but before sunset I had the satisfaction of knowing that there must be at least twenty-five miles between us and those accursed Zulus. Little Tota slept most of the way, the motion of the horse was easy, and she was worn out.

At last the sunset came, and we off-saddled in a dell by the river. There was not much to eat, but I soaked some biscuit in water for Tota, and Indaba-zimbi and I made a scanty meal of biltong. When we had done I took off Tota's frock, wrapped her up in a blanket near the fire we had made, and lit a pipe. I sat there by the side of the sleeping orphaned child, and from my heart thanked Providence for saving her life and mine from the slaughter of that day. What a horrible experience it had been! It seemed like a nightmare to look back upon. And yet it was sober fact, one among those many tragedies which dotted the paths of the emigrant Boers with the bones of men, women, and children. These horrors are almost forgotten now; people living in Natal now, for instance, can scarcely realize that some forty years ago six hundred white people, many of them women and children, were thus massacred by the Impis of Dingaan. But it was so, and the name of the district, Weenen, or the Place of Weeping, will commemorate them for ever.

Then I fell to reflecting on the extraordinary adroitness old Indaba-zimbi had shown in saving my life. It appeared that he himself had lived among the Umtetwa Zulus in his earlier manhood, and was a noted rain-doctor and witch-finder. But when T'Chaka, Dingaan's brother, ordered a general massacre of the witch-finders, he alone had saved his life by his skill in magic, and ultimately fled south for reasons too long to set out here. When he heard, therefore, that the regiment was an Umtetwa regiment, which, leaving their wives and children, had broken away from Zululand to escape the cruelties of Dingaan; under pretence of spying on them, he took the bold course of going straight up to the chief, Sususa, and addressing him as his brother, which he was. The chief knew him at once, and so did the soldiers, for his fame was still great among them. Then he told them his cock and bull story about my being a white spirit, whose presence in the laager would render it invincible, and with the object of saving my life in the slaughter which he knew must ensue, agreed to charm me out of the laager and deliver me into their keeping. How the plan worked has already been told; it was a risky one; still, but for it my troubles would have been done with these many days.

So I lay and thought with a heart full of gratitude, and as I did so saw old Indaba-zimbi sitting by the fire and going through some mysterious performances with bones which he produced from his bag, and ashes mixed with water. I spoke to him and asked what he was about. He replied that he was tracing out the route that we should follow. I felt inclined to answer "bosh!" but remembering the very remarkable instances which he had given of his prowess in occult matters I held my tongue, and taking little Tota into my arms, worn out with toil and danger and emotion, I went to sleep.

I awoke just as the dawn was beginning to flame across the sky in sheets of primrose and of gold, or rather it was little Tota who woke me by kissing me as she lay between sleep and waking, and calling me "papa." It wrung my heart to hear her, poor orphaned child. I got up, washed and dressed her as best I could, and we breakfasted as we had supped, on biltong and biscuit. Tota asked for milk, but I had none to give her. Then we caught the horses, and I saddled mine.

"Well, Indaba-zimbi," I said, "now what path do your bones point to?"

"Straight north," he said. "The journey will be hard, but in about four days we shall come to the kraal of a white man, an Englishman, not a Boer. His kraal is in a beautiful place, and there is a great peak behind it where there are many baboons."

I looked at him. "This is all nonsense, Indaba-zimbi," I said. "Whoever heard of an Englishman building a house in these wilds, and how do you know anything about it? I think that we had better strike east towards Port Natal."

"As you like, Macumazahn," he answered, "but it will take us three months' journey to get to Port Natal, if we ever get there, and the child will die on the road. Say, Macumazahn, have my words come true heretofore, or have they not? Did I not tell you not to hunt the elephants on horseback? Did I not tell you to take one waggon with you instead of two, as it is better to lose one than two?"

"You told me all these things," I answered.

"And so I tell you now to ride north, Macumazahn, for there you will find great happiness--yes, and great sorrow. But no man should run away from happiness because of the sorrow. As you will, as you will!"

Again I looked at him. In his divinations I did not believe, yet I came to the conclusion that he was speaking what he knew to be the truth. It struck me as possible that he might have heard of some white man living like a hermit in the wilds, but preferring to keep up his prophetic character would not say so.

"Very well, Indaba-zimbi," I said, "let us ride north."

Shortly after we started, the river we had followed hitherto turned off in a westerly direction, so we left it. All that day we rode across rolling uplands, and about an hour before sunset halted at a little stream which ran down from a range of hills in front of us. By this time I was heartily tired of the biltong, so taking my elephant rifle--for I had nothing else--I left Tota with Indaba-zimbi, and started to try if I could shoot something. Oddly enough we had seen no game all the day, nor did we see any on the subsequent days. For some mysterious reason they had temporarily left the district. I crossed the little streamlet in order to enter the belt of thorns which grew upon the hill-side beyond, for there I hoped to find buck. As I did so I was rather disturbed to see the spoor of two lions in the soft sandy edge of a pool. Breathing a hope that they might not still be in the neighbourhood, I went on into the belt of scattered thorns. For a long while I hunted about without seeing anything, except one duiker buck, which bounded off with a crash from the other side of a stone without giving me a chance. At length, just as it grew dusk, I spied a Petie buck, a graceful little creature, scarcely bigger than a large hare, standing on a stone, about forty yards from me. Under ordinary circumstances I should never have dreamed

87

of firing at such a thing, especially with an elephant gun, but we were hungry. So I sat down with my back against a rock, and aimed steadily at its head. I did this because if I struck it in the body the three-ounce ball would have knocked it to bits. At last I pulled the trigger, the gun went off with the report of a small cannon, and the buck disappeared. I ran to the spot with more anxiety than I should have felt in an ordinary way over a koodoo or an eland. To my delight there the little creature lay--the huge bullet had decapitated it. Considering all the circumstances I do not think I have often made a better shot than this, but if any one doubts, let him try his hand at a rabbit's head fifty yards away with an elephant gun and a three-ounce ball.

I picked up the Petie in triumph, and returned to the camp. There we skinned him and toasted his flesh over the fire. He just made a good meal for us, though we kept the hind legs for breakfast.

There was no moon this night, and so it chanced that when I suddenly remembered about the lion spoor, and suggested that we had better tie up the horses quite close to us, we could not find them, though we knew they were grazing within fifty yards. This being so we could only make up the fire and take our chance. Shortly afterwards I went to sleep with little Tota in my arms. Suddenly I was awakened by hearing that peculiarly painful sound, the scream of a horse, quite close to the fire, which was still burning brightly. Next second there came a noise of galloping hoofs, and before I could even rise my poor horse appeared in the ring of firelight. As in a flash of lightning I saw his staring eyes and wide-stretched nostrils, and the broken reim with which he had been knee-haltered, flying in the air. Also I saw something else, for on his back was a great dark form with glowing eyes, and from the form came a growling sound. It was a lion.

The horse dashed on. He galloped right through the fire, for which he had run in his terror, fortunately, however, without treading on us, and vanished into the night. We heard his hoofs for a hundred yards or more, then there was silence, broken now and again by distant growls. As may be imagined, we did not sleep any more that night, but waited anxiously till the dawn broke, two hours later.

As soon as there was sufficient light we rose, and, leaving Tota still asleep, crept cautiously in the direction in which the horse had vanished. When we had gone fifty yards or so, we made out its remains lying on the veldt, and caught sight of two great cat-like forms slinking away in the grey light.

To go any further was useless; we knew all about it now, so we turned to look for the other horse. But our cup of misfortune was not yet full; the horse was nowhere to be found. Terrified by the sight and smell of the lions, it had with a desperate effort also burst the reim with which it had been knee-haltered, and galloped far away. I sat down, feeling as though I could cry like a woman. For now we were left alone in these vast solitudes without a horse to carry us, and with a child who was not old enough to walk for more than a little way at a time.

Well, it was no use giving in, so with a few words we went back to our camp, where I found Tota crying because she had woke to find herself alone. Then we ate a little food and prepared to start. First we divided such articles as we must take with us into two equal parts, rejecting everything that we could possibly do without. Then, by an afterthought, we filled our water-bottles, though at the time I was rather against doing so, because of the extra weight. But Indaba-zimbi overruled me in the matter, fortunately for all three of us. I settled to look after Tota for the first march, and to give the elephant gun to Indaba-zimbi. At length all was ready, and we set out on foot. By the help of occasional lifts over rough places, Tota managed to walk up the slope of the hill-side where I had shot the Petie buck. At length we reached it, and, looking at the country beyond, I gave an exclamation of dismay. To say that it was desert would be saying too much; it was more like the Karroo in the Cape--a vast sandy waste, studded here and there with low shrubs and scattered rocks. But it was a great expanse of desolate land, stretching further than the eye could reach, and bordered far away by a line of purple hills, in the centre of which a great solitary peak soared high into the air.

"Indaba-zimbi," I said, "we can never cross this if we take six days."

"As you will, Macumazahn," he answered; "but I tell you that there"--and he pointed to the peak--"there the white man lives. Turn which way you like, but if you turn you will perish."

I reflected for a moment, Our case was, humanly speaking, almost hopeless. It mattered little which way we went. We were alone, almost without food, with no means of transport, and a child to carry. As well perish in the sandy waste as on the rolling veldt or among the trees of the hill-side. Providence alone could save us, and we must trust to Providence.

"Come on," I said, lifting Tota on to my back, for she was already tired. "All roads lead to rest."

How am I to describe the misery of the next four days? How am I to tell how we stumbled on through that awful desert, almost without food, and quite without water, for there were no streams, and we saw no springs? We soon found how the case was, and saved almost all the water in our bottles for the child. To look back on it is like a nightmare. I can scarcely bear to dwell on it. Day after day, by turns carrying the child through the heavy sand; night after night lying down in the scrub, chewing the leaves, and licking such dew as there was from the scanty grass! Not a spring, not a pool, not a head of game! It was the third night; we were nearly mad with thirst. Tota was in a comatose condition. Indaba-zimbi still had a little water in his bottle--perhaps a wine-glassful. With it we moistened our lips and blackened tongues. Then we gave the rest to the child. It revived her. She awoke from her swoon to sink into sleep.

91

See, the dawn was breaking. The hills were not more than eight miles or so away now, and they were green. There must be water there.

"Come," I said.

Indaba-zimbi lifted Tota into the kind of sling that we had made out of the blanket in which to carry her on our backs, and we staggered on for an hour through the sand. She awoke crying for water, and alas! we had none to give her; our tongues were hanging from our lips, we could scarcely speak.

We rested awhile, and Tota mercifully swooned away again. Then Indaba-zimbi took her. Though he was so thin the old man's strength was wonderful.

Another hour; the slope of the great peak could not be more than two miles away now. A couple of hundred yards off grew a large baobab tree. Could we reach its shade? We had done half the distance when Indaba-zimbi fell from exhaustion. We were now so weak that neither of us could lift the child on to our backs. He rose again, and we each took one of her hands and dragged her along the road. Fifty yards--they seemed to be fifty miles. Ah, the tree was reached at last; compared with the heat outside, the shade of its dense foliage seemed like the dusk and cool of a vault. I remember thinking that it was a good place to die in. Then I remember no more.

I woke with a feeling as though the blessed rain were falling on my face and head. Slowly, and with great difficulty, I opened my eyes, then shut them again, having seen a vision. For a space I lay thus, while the rain continued to fall; I saw now that I must be asleep, or off my head with thirst and fever. If I were not off my head how came I to imagine that a lovely dark-eyed girl was bending over me sprinkling water on my face? A white girl, too, not a Kaffir woman. However, the dream went on.

"Hendrika," said a voice in English, the sweetest voice that I had ever heard; somehow it reminded me of wind whispering in the trees at night. "Hendrika, I fear he dies; there is a flask of brandy in my saddle-bag; get it."

"Ah! ah!" grunted a harsh voice in answer; "let him die, Miss Stella. He will bring you bad luck--let him die, I say." I felt a movement of air above me as though the woman of my vision turned swiftly, and once again I opened my eyes. She had risen, this dream woman. Now I saw that she was tall and graceful as a reed. She was angry, too; her dark eyes flashed, and she pointed with her hand at a female who stood before her, dressed in nondescript kind of clothes such as might be worn by either a man or a woman. The woman was young, of white blood, very short, with bowed legs and enormous shoulders. In face she was not bad-looking, but the brow receded, the chin and ears were prominent--in short, she reminded me of nothing so much as a very handsome monkey. She might have

93

been the missing link.

The lady was pointing at her with her hand. "How dare you?" she said. "Are you going to disobey me again? Have you forgotten what I told you, Babyan?"[*]

[*] Baboon.

"Ah! ah!" grunted the woman, who seemed literally to curl and shrivel up beneath her anger. "Don't be angry with me, Miss Stella, because I can't bear it. I only said it because it was true. I will fetch the brandy."

Then, dream or no dream, I determined to speak.

"Not brandy," I gasped in English as well as my swollen tongue would allow; "give me water."

"Ah, he lives!" cried the beautiful girl, "and he talks English. See, sir, here is water in your own bottle; you were quite close to a spring, it is on the other side of the tree."

I struggled to a sitting position, lifted the bottle to my lips, and drank from it. Oh! that drink of cool, pure water! never had I tasted anything so delicious. With the first gulp I felt life flow back into me. But wisely enough she would not let me have much. "No more! no more!" she said, and dragged the bottle from me almost by force.

"The child," I said--"is the child dead?"

"I do not know yet," she answered. "We have only just found you, and I tried to revive you first."

I turned and crept to where Tota lay by the side of Indaba-zimbi. It was impossible to say if they were dead or swooning. The lady sprinkled Tota's face with the water, which I watched greedily, for my thirst was still awful, while the woman Hendrika did the same office for Indaba-zimbi. Presently, to my vast delight, Tota opened her eyes and tried to cry, but could not, poor little thing, because her tongue and lips were so swollen. But the lady got some water into her mouth, and, as in my case, the effect was magical. We allowed her to drink about a quarter of a pint, and no more, though she cried bitterly for it. Just then old Indaba-zimbi came to with a groan. He opened his eyes, glanced round, and took in the situation.

"What did I tell you, Macumazahn?" he gasped, and seizing the bottle, he took a long pull at it.

Meanwhile I sat with my back against the trunk of the great tree and tried to realize the situation. Looking to my left I saw too good horses--one bare-backed, and one with a rudely made lady's saddle on it. By the side of the horses were two dogs, of a stout greyhound breed, that sat watching us, and near the dogs lay a dead Oribé buck, which

95

they had evidently been coursing.

"Hendrika," said the lady presently, "they must not eat meat just yet. Go look up the tree and see if there is any ripe fruit on it."

The woman ran swiftly into the plain and obeyed. Presently she returned. "I see some ripe fruit," she said, "but it is high, quite at the top."

"Fetch it," said the lady.

"Easier said than done," I thought to myself; but I was much mistaken. Suddenly the woman bounded at least three feet into the air and caught one of the spreading boughs in her large flat hands; then came a swing that would have filled an acrobat with envy--and she was on it.

"Now there is an end," I thought again, for the next bough was beyond her reach. But again I was mistaken. She stood up on the bough, gripping it with her bare feet, and once more sprang at the one above, caught it and swung herself into it.

I suppose that the lady saw my expression of astonishment. "Do not wonder, sir," she said, "Hendrika is not like other people. She will not fall."

I made no answer, but watched the progress of this extraordinary person with the most breathless interest. On she went, swinging herself from bough to bough, and running along them like a monkey. At last she reached the top, and began to swarm up a thin branch towards the ripe fruit. When she was near enough she shook the branch violently. There was a crack--a crash--it broke. I shut my eyes, expecting to see her crushed on the ground before me.

"Don't be afraid," said the lady again, laughing gently. "Look, she is quite safe."

I looked, and so she was. She had caught a bough as she fell, clung to it, and was now calmly dropping to another. Old Indaba-zimbi had also watched this performance with interest, but it did not seem to astonish him over-much. "Baboon-woman?" he said, as though such people were common, and then turned his attention to soothing Tota, who was moaning for more water. Meanwhile Hendrika came down the tree with extraordinary rapidity, and swinging by one hand from a bough, dropped about eight feet to the ground.

In another two minutes we were all three sucking the pulpy fruit. In an ordinary way we should have found it tasteless enough: as it was I thought it the most delicious thing I had ever tasted. After three days spent without food or water, in the desert, one is not particular. While we were still eating the fruit, the lady of my vision set her companion to work to partially flay the oribé which her dogs had killed, and busied herself in making a fire of fallen boughs. As soon as it burned brightly she took strips of the oribé flesh, toasted them, and gave them

97

to us on leaves. We ate, and now were allowed a little more water. After
that she took Tota to the spring and washed her, which she sadly needed,
poor child! Next came our turn to wash, and oh, the joy of it!

I came back to the tree, walking painfully, indeed, but a changed man.
There sat the beautiful girl with Tota on her knees. She was lulling her
to sleep, and held up her finger to me enjoining silence. At last the
child went off into a sound natural slumber--an example that I should
have been glad to follow had it not been for my burning curiosity. Then
I spoke.

"May I ask what your name is?" I said.

"Stella," she answered.

"Stella what?" I said.

"Stella nothing," she answered, in some pique; "Stella is my name; it is
short and easy to remember at any rate. My father's name is Thomas, and
we live up there," and she pointed round the base of the great peak. I
looked at her astonished. "Have you lived there long?" I asked.

"Ever since I was seven years old. We came there in a waggon. Before
that we came from England--from Oxfordshire; I can show you the place on
a big map. It is called Garsingham."

Again I thought I must be dreaming. "Do you know, Miss Stella," I said, "it is very strange--so strange that it almost seems as though it could not be true--but I also came from Garsingham in Oxfordshire many years ago."

She started up. "Are you an English gentleman?" she said. "Ah, I have always longed to see an English gentleman. I have never seen but one Englishman since we lived here, and he certainly was not a gentleman--no white people at all, indeed, except a few wandering Boers. We live among black people and baboons--only I have read about English people--lots of books--poetry and novels. But tell me what is your name? Macumazahn the black man called you, but you must have a white name, too."

"My name is Allan Quatermain," I said.

Her face turned quite white, her rosy lips parted, and she looked at me wildly with her beautiful dark eyes.

"It is wonderful," she said, "but I have often heard that name. My father has told me how a little boy called Allan Quatermain once saved my life by putting out my dress when it was on fire--see!"--and she pointed to a faint red mark upon her neck--"here is the scar of the burn."

"I remember it," I said. "You were dressed up as Father Christmas. It was I who put out the fire; my wrists were burnt in doing so."

99

Then for a space we sat silent, looking at each other, while Stella slowly fanned herself with her wide felt hat, in which some white ostrich plumes were fixed.

"This is God's doing," she said at last. "You saved my life when I was a child; now I have saved yours and the little girl's. Is she your own daughter?" she added, quickly.

"No," I answered; "I will tell you the tale presently."

"Yes," she said, "you shall tell me as we go home. It is time to be starting home, it will take us three hours to get there. Hendrika, Hendrika, bring the horses here!"

CHAPTER VII

THE BABOON-WOMAN

Hendrika obeyed, leading the horses to the side of the tree.

"Now, Mr. Allan," said Stella, "you must ride on my horse, and the old black man must ride on the other. I will walk, and Hendrika will carry the child. Oh, do not be afraid, she is very strong, she could carry you or me."

Hendrika grunted assent. I am sorry that I cannot express her method of speech by any more polite term. Sometimes she grunted like a monkey, sometimes she clicked like a Bushman, and sometimes she did both together, when she became quite unintelligible.

I expostulated against this proposed arrangement, saying that we could walk, which was a fib, for I do not think that I could have done a mile; but Stella would not listen, she would not even let me carry my elephant gun, but took it herself. So we mounted with some difficulty, and Hendrika took up the sleeping Tota in her long, sinewy arms.

"See that the 'Baboon-woman' does not run away into the mountains with the little white one," said Indaba-zimbi to me in Kaffir, as he climbed slowly on to the horse.

Unfortunately Hendrika understood his speech. Her face twisted and grew livid with fury. She put down Tota and literally sprang at Indaba-zimbi as a monkey springs. But weary and worn as he was, the old gentleman was too quick for her. With an exclamation of genuine fright he threw himself from the horse on the further side, with the somewhat ludicrous result that all in a moment Hendrika was occupying the seat which he had vacated. Just then Stella realized the position.

"Come down, you savage, come down!" she said, stamping her foot.

The extraordinary creature flung herself from the horse and literally grovelled on the ground before her mistress and burst into tears.

"Pardon, Miss Stella," she clicked and grunted in villainous English, "but he called me 'Babyan-frau' (Baboon-woman)."

"Tell your servant that he must not use such words to Hendrika, Mr. Allan," Stella said to me. "If he does," she added, in a whisper, "Hendrika will certainly kill him."

I explained this to Indaba-zimbi, who, being considerably frightened, deigned to apologize. But from that hour there was hate and war between these two.

Harmony having been thus restored, we started, the dogs following us. A small strip of desert intervened between us and the slope of the peak--perhaps it was two miles wide. We crossed it and reached rich grass lands, for here a considerable stream gathered from the hills; but it did not flow across the barren lands, it passed to the east along the foot of the hills. This stream we had to cross by a ford. Hendrika walked boldly through it, holding Tota in her arms. Stella leapt across from stone to stone like a roebuck; I thought to myself that she was the most graceful creature that I had ever seen. After this the track passed around a pleasantly-wooded shoulder of the peak, which was, I found, known as Babyan Kap, or Baboon Head. Of course we could only go at a foot pace, so our progress was slow. Stella walked for some way in silence, then she spoke.

"Tell me, Mr. Allan," she said, "how it was that I came to find you dying in the desert?"

So I began and told her all. It took an hour or more to do so, and she listened intently, now and again asking a question.

"It is all very wonderful," she said when I had done, "very wonderful indeed. Do you know I went out this morning with Hendrika and the dogs for a ride, meaning to get back home by mid-day, for my father is ill, and I do not like to leave him for long. But just as I was going to turn, when we were about where we are now--yes, that was the very bush--an oribé got up, and the dogs chased it. I followed them for the gallop, and when we came to the river, instead of turning to the left as bucks generally do, the oribé swam the stream and took to the Bad Lands

103

beyond. I followed it, and within a hundred yards of the big tree the dogs killed it. Hendrika wanted to turn back at once, but I said that we would rest under the shade of the tree, for I knew that there was a spring of water near. Well, we went; and there I saw you all lying like dead; but Hendrika, who is very clever in some ways, said no--and you know the rest. Yes, it is very wonderful."

"It is indeed," I said. "Now tell me, Miss Stella, who is Hendrika?"

She looked round before answering to see that the woman was not near.

"Hers is a strange story, Mr. Allan. I will tell you. You must know that all these mountains and the country beyond are full of baboons. When I was a girl of about ten I used to wander a great deal alone in the hills and valleys, and watch the baboons as they played among the rocks. There was one family of baboons that I watched especially--they used to live in a kloof about a mile from the house. The old man baboon was very large, and one of the females had a grey face. But the reason why I watched them so much was because I saw that they had with them a creature that looked like a girl, for her skin was quite white, and, what was more, that she was protected from the weather when it happened to be cold by a fur belt of some sort, which was tied round her throat. The old baboons seemed to be especially fond of her, and would sit with their arms round her neck. For nearly a whole summer I watched this particular white-skinned baboon till at last my curiosity quite overmastered me. I noticed that, though she climbed about the cliffs with the other monkeys, at a certain hour a little before sundown they used to put her with one or two other much smaller ones into a little cave, while the family went off somewhere to get food, to the mealie fields, I suppose. Then I got an idea that I would catch this white baboon and bring it home. But of course I could not do this by myself, so I took a Hottentot--a very clever man when he was not drunk--who lived on the stead, into my confidence. He was called Hendrik, and was very fond of me; but for a long while he would not listen to my plan, because he said that the babyans would kill us. At last I bribed him with a knife that had four blades, and one afternoon we started, Hendrik carrying a stout sack made of hide, with a rope running through it so that the mouth could be drawn tight.

"Well, we got to the place, and, hiding ourselves carefully in the trees at the foot of the kloof, watched the baboons playing about and grunting to each other, till at length, according to custom, they took the white one and three other little babies and put them in the cave. Then the old man came out, looked carefully round, called to his family, and went off with them over the brow of the kloof. Now very slowly and cautiously we crept up over the rocks till we came to the mouth of the cave and looked in. All the four little baboons were fast asleep, with their backs towards us, and their arms round each other's necks, the white one being in the middle. Nothing could have been better for our plans. Hendrik, who by this time had quite entered into the spirit of the thing, crept along the cave like a snake, and suddenly dropped the mouth of the hide bag over the head of the white baboon. The poor little thing woke up and gave a violent jump which caused it to vanish right into the bag. Then Hendrik pulled the string tight, and together we knotted it so that it was impossible for our captive to escape. Meanwhile the other baby baboons had rushed from the cave screaming, and when we got outside they were nowhere to be seen.

"'Come on, Missie,' said Hendrik; 'the babyans will soon be back.' He had shouldered the sack, inside of which the white baboon was kicking violently, and screaming like a child. It was dreadful to hear its shrieks.

"We scrambled down the sides of the kloof and ran for home as fast as we could manage. When we were near the waterfall, and within about three hundred yards of the garden wall, we heard a voice behind us, and there, leaping from rock to rock, and running over the grass, was the whole family of baboons headed by the old man.

"'Run, Missie, run!' gasped Hendrik, and I did, like the wind, leaving him far behind. I dashed into the garden, where some Kaffirs were working, crying, 'The babyans! the babyans!' Luckily the men had their sticks and spears by them and ran out just in time to save Hendrik, who was almost overtaken. The baboons made a good fight for it, however, and it was not till the old man was killed with an assegai that they ran away.

"Well, there is a stone hut in the kraal at the stead where my father sometimes shuts up natives who have misbehaved. It is very strong, and has a barred window. To this hut Hendrik carried the sack, and, having untied the mouth, put it down on the floor, and ran from the place, shutting the door behind him. In another moment the poor little thing was out and dashing round the stone hut as though it were mad. It sprung at the bars of the window, clung there, and beat its head against them till the blood came. Then it fell to the floor, and sat upon it crying like a child, and rocking itself backwards and forwards. It was so sad to see it that I began to cry too.

"Just then my father came in and asked what all the fuss was about. I told him that we had caught a young white baboon, and he was angry, and said that it must be let go. But when he looked at it through the bars of the window he nearly fell down with astonishment.

"'Why!' he said, 'this is not a baboon, it is a white child that the baboons have stolen and brought up!'

"Now, Mr. Allan, whether my father is right or wrong, you can judge for yourself. You see Hendrika--we named her that after Hendrik, who caught her--she is a woman, not a monkey, and yet she has many of the ways of monkeys, and looks like one too. You saw how she can climb, for instance, and you hear how she talks. Also she is very savage, and when she is angry or jealous she seems to go mad, though she is as clever as anybody. I think that she must have been stolen by the baboons when she was quite tiny and nurtured by them, and that is why she is so like them.

"But to go on. My father said that it was our duty to keep Hendrika at any cost. The worst of it was, that for three days she would eat nothing, and I thought that she would die, for all the while she sat and wailed. On the third day, however, I went to the bars of the window place, and held out a cup of milk and some fruit to her. She looked at it for a long while, then crept up moaning, took the milk from my hand, drank it greedily, and afterwards ate the fruit. From that time forward she took food readily enough, but only if I would feed her.

"But I must tell you of the dreadful end of Hendrik. From the day that we captured Hendrika the whole place began to swarm with baboons which were evidently employed in watching the kraals. One day Hendrik went out towards the hills alone to gather some medicine. He did not come back again, so the next day search was made. By a big rock which I can show you, they found his scattered and broken bones, the fragments of his assegai, and four dead baboons. They had set upon him and torn him to pieces.

"My father was very much frightened at this, but still he would not let Hendrika go, because he said that she was human, and that it was our duty to reclaim her. And so we did--to a certain extent, at least. After the murder of Hendrik, the baboons vanished from the neighbourhood, and have only returned quite recently, so at length we ventured to let Hendrika out. By this time she had grown very fond of me; still, on the first opportunity she ran away. But in the evening she returned again. She had been seeking the baboons, and could not find them. Shortly afterwards she began to speak--I taught her--and from that time she has loved me so that she will not leave me. I think it would kill her if I went away from her. She watches me all day, and at night sleeps on the floor of my hut. Once, too, she saved my life when I was swept down the river in flood; but she is jealous, and hates everybody else. Look, how she is glaring at you now because I am talking to you!"

I looked. Hendrika was tramping along with the child in her arms and staring at me in a most sinister fashion out of the corners of her eyes.

While I was reflecting on the Baboon-woman's strange story, and thinking that she was an exceedingly awkward customer, the path took a sudden turn.

"Look!" said Stella, "there is our home. Is it not beautiful?"

It was beautiful indeed. Here on the western side of the great peak a bay had been formed in the mountain, which might have measured eight hundred or a thousand yards across by three-quarters of a mile in depth. At the back of this indentation the sheer cliff rose to the height of several hundred feet, and behind it and above it the great Babyan Peak towered up towards the heavens. The space of ground, embraced thus in the arms of the mountain, as it were, was laid out, as though by the cunning hand of man, in three terraces that rose one above the other. To

the right and left of the topmost terrace were chasms in the cliff, and
down each chasm fell a waterfall, from no great height, indeed, but of
considerable volume. These two streams flowed away on either side of
the enclosed space, one towards the north, and the other, the course
of which we had been following, round the base of the mountain. At each
terrace they made a cascade, so that the traveller approaching had a
view of eight waterfalls at once. Along the edge of the stream to our
left were placed Kaffir kraals, built in orderly groups with verandahs,
after the Basutu fashion, and a very large part of the entire space of
land was under cultivation. All of this I noted at once, as well as the
extraordinary richness and depth of the soil, which for many ages past
had been washed down from the mountain heights. Then following the line
of an excellent waggon road, on which we now found ourselves, that wound
up from terrace to terrace, my eye lit upon the crowning wonder of the
scene. For in the centre of the topmost platform or terrace, which may
have enclosed eight or ten acres of ground, and almost surrounded by
groves of orange trees, gleamed buildings of which I had never seen the
like. There were three groups of them, one in the middle, and one on
either side, and a little to the rear, but, as I afterwards discovered,
the plan of all was the same. In the centre was an edifice constructed
like an ordinary Zulu hut--that is to say, in the shape of a beehive,
only it was five times the size of any hut I ever saw, and built
of blocks of hewn white marble, fitted together with extraordinary
knowledge of the principles and properties of arch building, and with so
much accuracy and finish that it was often difficult to find the joints
of the massive blocks. From this centre hut ran three covered passages,

leading to other buildings of an exactly similar character, only smaller, and each whole block was enclosed by a marble wall about four feet in height.

Of course we were as yet too far off to see all these details, but the general outline I saw at once, and it astonished me considerably. Even old Indaba-zimbi, whom the Baboon-woman had been unable to move, deigned to show wonder.

"Ou!" he said; "this is a place of marvels. Who ever saw kraals built of white stone?"

Stella watched our faces with an expression of intense amusement, but said nothing.

"Did your father build those kraals?" I gasped, at length.

"My father! no, of course not," she answered. "How would it have been possible for one white man to do so, or to have made this road? He found them as you see."

"Who built them, then?" I said again.

"I do not know. My father thinks that they are very ancient, for the people who live here now do not know how to lay one stone upon another, and these huts are so wonderfully constructed that, though they must

111

have stood for ages, not a stone of them had fallen. But I can show you the quarry where the marble was cut; it is close by and behind it is the entrance to an ancient mine, which my father thinks was a silver mine. Perhaps the people who worked the mine built the marble huts. The world is old, and no doubt plenty of people have lived in it and been forgotten."[*]

[*] Kraals of a somewhat similar nature to those described by Mr. Quatermain have been discovered in the Marico district of the Transvaal, and an illustration of them is to be found in Mr. Anderson's "Twenty-five Years in a Waggon," vol. ii. p. 55. Mr. Anderson says, "In this district are the ancient stone kraals mentioned in an early chapter; but it requires a fuller description to show that these extensive kraals must have been erected by a white race who understood building in stone and at right angles, with door-posts, lintels, and sills, and it required more than Kaffir skill to erect the stone huts, with stone circular roofs, beautifully formed and most substantially erected; strong enough, if not disturbed, to last a thousand years." --Editor.

Then we rode on in silence. I have seen many beautiful sights in Africa, and in such matters, as in others, comparisons are odious and worthless, but I do not think that I ever saw a lovelier scene. It was no one thing--it was the combination of the mighty peak looking forth on to the

everlasting plains, the great cliffs, the waterfalls that sparkled
in rainbow hues, the rivers girdling the rich cultivated lands, the
gold-specked green of the orange trees, the flashing domes of the marble
huts, and a thousand other things. Then over all brooded the peace of
evening, and the infinite glory of the sunset that filled heaven with
changing hues of splendour, that wrapped the mountain and cliffs in
cloaks of purple and of gold, and lay upon the quiet face of the water
like the smile of a god.

Perhaps also the contrast, and the memory of those three awful days
and nights in the hopeless desert, enhanced the charm, and perhaps the
beauty of the girl who walked beside me completed it. For of this I am
sure, that of all sweet and lovely things that I looked on then, she was
the sweetest and the loveliest.

Ah, it did not take me long to find my fate. How long will it be before
I find her once again?

CHAPTER VIII

THE MARBLE KRAALS

At length the last platform, or terrace, was reached, and we pulled up
outside the wall surrounding the central group of marble huts--for so
I must call them, for want of a better name. Our approach had been
observed by a crowd of natives, whose race I have never been able to
determine accurately; they belonged to the Basutu and peaceful section
of the Bantu peoples rather than to the Zulu and warlike. Several of
these ran up to take the horses, gazing on us with astonishment, not
unmixed with awe. We dismounted--speaking for myself, not without
difficulty--indeed, had it not been for Stella's support I should have
fallen.

"Now you must come and see my father," she said. "I wonder what he will
think of it, it is all so strange. Hendrika, take the child to my hut
and give her milk, then put her into my bed; I will come presently."

Hendrika went off with a somewhat ugly grin to do her mistress's
bidding, and Stella led the way through the narrow gateway in the marble
wall, which may have enclosed nearly half an "erf," or three-quarters of
an acre of ground in all. It was beautifully planted as a garden, many
European vegetables and flowers were growing in it, besides others with
which I was not acquainted. Presently we came to the centre hut, and
it was then that I noticed the extraordinary beauty and finish of the

114

marble masonry. In the hut, and facing the gateway, was a modern door, rather rudely fashioned of Buckenhout, a beautiful reddish wood that has the appearance of having been sedulously pricked with a pin. Stella opened it, and we entered. The interior of the hut was the size of a large and lofty room, the walls being formed of plain polished marble. It was lighted somewhat dimly, but quite effectively, by peculiar openings in the roof, from which the rain was excluded by overhanging eaves. The marble floor was strewn with native mats and skins of animals. Bookcases filled with books were placed against the walls, there was a table in the centre, chairs seated with rimpi or strips of hide stood about, and beyond the table was a couch on which a man was lying reading.

"Is that you, Stella?" said a voice, that even after so many years seemed familiar to me. "Where have you been, my dear? I began to think that you had lost yourself again."

"No, father, dear, I have not lost myself, but I have found somebody else."

At that moment I stepped forward so that the light fell on me. The old gentleman on the couch rose with some difficulty and bowed with much courtesy. He was a fine-looking old man, with deep-set dark eyes, a pale face that bore many traces of physical and mental suffering, and a long white beard.

"Be welcome, sir," he said. "It is long since we have seen a white face in these wilds, and yours, if I am not mistaken, is that of an Englishman. There has been but one Englishman here for twelve years, and he, I grieve to say, was an outcast flying from justice," and he bowed again and stretched out his hand.

I looked at him, and then of a sudden his name flashed back into my mind. I took his hand.

"How do you do, Mr. Carson?" I said.

He started as though he had been stung.

"Who told you that name?" he cried. "It is a dead name. Stella, is it you? I forbade you to let it pass your lips."

"I did not speak it, father. I have never spoken it," she answered.

"Sir," I broke in, "if you will allow me I will show you how I came to know your name. Do you remember many years ago coming into the study of a clergyman in Oxfordshire and telling him that you were going to leave England for ever?"

He bowed his head.

"And do you remember a little boy who sat upon the hearthrug writing with a pencil?"

"I do," he said.

"Sir, I was that boy, and my name is Allan Quatermain. Those children
who lay sick are all dead, their mother is dead, and my father, your old
friend, is dead also. Like you he emigrated, and last year he died in
the Cape. But that is not all the story. After many adventures, I, one
Kaffir, and a little girl, lay senseless and dying in the Bad Lands,
where we had wandered for days without water, and there we should have
perished, but your daughter, Miss----"

"Call her Stella," he broke in, hastily. "I cannot bear to hear that
name. I have forsworn it."

"Miss Stella found us by chance and saved our lives."

"By chance, did you say, Allan Quatermain?" he answered. "There is
little chance in all this; such chances spring from another will than
ours. Welcome, Allan, son of my old friend. Here we live as it were in a
hermitage, with Nature as our only friend, but such as we have is yours,
and for as long as you will take it. But you must be starving; talk no
more now. Stella, it is time to eat. To-morrow we will talk."

To tell the truth I can recall very little of the events of that
evening. A kind of dizzy weariness overmastered me. I remember sitting

117

at a table next to Stella, and eating heartily, and then I remember nothing more.

I awoke to find myself lying on a comfortable bed in a hut built and fashioned on the same model as the centre one. While I was wondering what time it was, a native came bringing some clean clothes on his arm, and, luxury of luxuries, produced a bath hollowed from wood. I rose, feeling a very different man, my strength had come back again to me; I dressed, and following a covered passage found myself in the centre hut. Here the table was set for breakfast with all manner of good things, such as I had not seen for many a month, which I contemplated with healthy satisfaction. Presently I looked up, and there before me was a more delightful sight, for standing in one of the doorways which led to the sleeping huts was Stella, leading little Tota by the hand.

She was very simply dressed in a loose blue gown, with a wide collar, and girdled in at the waist by a little leather belt. In the bosom of her robe was a bunch of orange blooms, and her rippling hair was tied in a single knot behind her shapely head. She greeted me with a smile, asking how I had slept, and then held Tota up for me to kiss. Under her loving care the child had been quite transformed. She was neatly dressed in a garment of the same blue stuff that Stella wore, her fair hair was brushed; indeed, had it not been for the sun blisters on her face and hands, one would scarcely have believed that this was the same child whom Indaba-zimbi and I had dragged for hour after hour through the burning, waterless desert.

118

"We must breakfast alone, Mr. Allan," she said; "my father is so upset by your arrival that he will not get up yet. Oh, you cannot tell how thankful I am that you have come. I have been so anxious about him of late. He grows weaker and weaker; it seems to me as though the strength were ebbing away from him. Now he scarcely leaves the kraal, I have to manage everything about the farm; he does nothing but read and think."

Just then Hendrika entered, bearing a jug of coffee in one hand and of milk in the other, which she set down upon the table, casting a look of little love at me as she did so.

"Be careful, Hendrika; you are spilling the coffee," said Stella. "Don't you wonder how we come to have coffee here, Mr. Allan? I will tell you--we grow it. That was my idea. Oh, I have lots of things to show you. You don't know what we have managed to do in the time that we have been here. You see we have plenty of labour, for the people about look upon my father as their chief."

"Yes," I said, "but how do you get all these luxuries of civilization?" and I pointed to the books, the crockery, and the knives and forks.

"Very simply. Most of the books my father brought with him when we first trekked into the wilds; there was nearly a waggon load of them. But every few years we have sent an expedition of three waggons right down to Port Natal. The waggons are loaded with ivory and other goods, and come back with all kinds of things that been sent out from England for us. So you see, although we live in this wild place, we are not altogether cut off. We can send runners to Natal and back in three months, and the waggons get there and back in a year. The last lot arrived quite safe about three months ago. Our servants are very faithful, and some of them speak Dutch well."

"Have you ever been with the waggons?" I asked.

"Since I was a child I have never been more than thirty miles from Babyan's Peak," she answered. "Do you know, Mr. Allan, that you are, with one exception, the first Englishman that I have known out of a book. I suppose that I must seem very wild and savage to you, but I have had one advantage--a good education. My father has taught me everything, and perhaps I know some things that you don't. I can read French and German, for instance. I think that my father's first idea was to let me run wild altogether, but he gave it up."

"And don't you wish to go into the world?" I asked.

"Sometimes," she said, "when I get lonely. But perhaps my father is right--perhaps it would frighten and bewilder me. At any rate he would never return to civilization; it is his idea, you know, although I am sure I do not know where he got it from, nor why he cannot bear that our name should be spoken. In short, Mr. Quatermain, we do not make our lives, we must take them as we find them. Have you done your breakfast?

120

Let us go out, and I will show you our home."

I rose and went to my sleeping-place to fetch my hat. When I returned,
Mr. Carson--for after all that was his name, though he would never allow
it to be spoken--had come into the hut. He felt better now, he said, and
would accompany us on our walk if Stella would give him an arm.

So we started, and after us came Hendrika with Tota and old Indaba-zimbi
whom I found sitting outside as fresh as paint. Nothing could tire that
old man.

The view from the platform was almost as beautiful as that from the
lower ground looking up to the peak. The marble kraals, as I have said,
faced west, consequently all the upper terrace lay in the shadow of the
great peak till nearly eleven o'clock in the morning--a great advantage
in that warm latitude. First we walked through the garden, which was
beautifully cultivated, and one of the most productive that I ever saw.
There were three or four natives working in it, and they all saluted
my host as "Baba," or father. Then we visited the other two groups of
marble huts. One of these was used for stables and outbuildings, the
other as storehouses, the centre hut having been, however, turned into
a chapel. Mr. Carson was not ordained, but he earnestly tried to convert
the natives, most of whom were refugees who had come to him for shelter,
and he had practised the more elementary rites of the church for so long
that I think he began to believe that he really was a clergyman. For
instance, he always married those of his people who would consent to a

121

monogamous existence, and baptized their children.

When we had examined those wonderful remains of antiquity, the marble huts, and admired the orange trees, the vines and fruits which thrive like weeds in this marvellous soil and climate, we descended to the next platform, and saw the farming operations in full swing. I think that it was the best farm I have ever seen in Africa. There was ample water for purposes of irrigation, the grass lands below gave pasturage for hundreds of head of cattle and horses, and, for natives, the people were most industrious. Moreover, the whole place was managed by Mr. Carson on the co-operative system; he only took a tithe of the produce--indeed, in this land of teeming plenty, what was he to do with more? Consequently the tribesmen, who, by the way, called themselves the "Children of Thomas," were able to accumulate considerable wealth. All their disputes were referred to their "father," and he also was judge of offences and crimes. Some were punished by imprisonment, whipping, and loss of goods, other and graver transgressions by expulsion from the community, a fiat which to one of these favoured natives must have seemed as heavy as the decree that drove Adam from the Garden of Eden.

Old Mr. Carson leaned upon his daughter's arm and contemplated the scene with pride.

"I have done all this, Allan Quatermain," he said. "When renouncing civilization, I wandered here by chance; seeking a home in the remotest places of the world, I found this lonely spot a wilderness. Nothing was to be seen except the site, the domes of the marble huts, and the waterfalls. I took possession of the huts. I cleared the path of garden land and planted the orange grove. I had only six natives then, but by degrees others joined me, now my tribe is a thousand strong. Here we live in profound peace and plenty. I have all I need, and I seek no more. Heaven has prospered me so far--may it do so to the end, which for me draws nigh. And now I am tired and will go back. If you wish to see the old quarry and the mouth of the ancient mines, Stella will show them to you. No, my love, you need not trouble to come, I can manage. Look! some of the headmen are waiting to see me."

So he went; but still followed by Hendrika and Indaba-zimbi, we turned, and, walking along the bank of one of the rivers, passed up behind the marble kraals, and came to the quarry, whence the material of which they were built had been cut in some remote age. The pit opened up a very thick seam of the whitest and most beautiful marble. I know another like it in Natal. But by whom it had been worked I cannot say; not by natives, that is certain, though the builders of these kraals had condescended to borrow the shape of native huts for their model. By the way, the only relic of those builders that I ever saw was a highly finished bronze pick-axe which Stella had found one day in the quarry.

After we had examined this quarry we climbed the slope of the hill till we came to the mouth of the ancient mines which were situated in a gorge. I believe them to have been silver mines. The gorge was long and narrow, and the moment we entered it there rose from every side a sound

123

of groaning and barking that was almost enough to deafen us. I knew what it was at once: the whole place was filled with baboons, which clambered down the rocks towards us from every direction, and in a manner that struck me as being unnaturally fearless. Stella turned a little pale and clung to my arm.

"It is very silly of me," she whispered. "I am not at all nervous, but ever since they killed Hendrik I cannot bear the sight of those animals. I always think that there is something human about them."

Meanwhile the baboons drew nearer, talking to each other as they came. Tota began to cry, and clung to Stella. Stella clung to me, while I and Indaba-zimbi put as bold a front on the matter as we could. Only Hendrika stood looking at the brutes with an unconcerned smile on her monkey face. When the great apes were quite near, she suddenly called aloud. Instantly they stopped their hideous clamour as though at a word of command. Then Hendrika addressed them: I can only describe it so. That is to say, she began to make a noise such as baboons do when they converse with each other. I have known Hottentots and Bushmen who said that they could talk with the baboons and understand their language, but I confess I never heard it done before or since.

From the mouth of Hendrika came a succession of grunts, groans, squeals, clicks, and every other abominable noise that can be conceived, conveying to my mind a general idea of expostulation. At any rate the baboons listened. One of them grunted back some answer, and then the

124

whole mob drew off to the rocks.

I stood astonished, and without a word we turned back to the kraal, for Hendrika was too close to allow me to speak. When we reached the dining hut Stella went in, followed by Hendrika. But Indaba-zimbi plucked me by the sleeve, and I stopped outside.

"Macumazahn," he said. "Baboon-woman--devil-woman. Be careful, Macumazahn. She loves that Star (the natives aptly enough called Stella the Star), and is jealous. Be careful, Macumazahn, or the Star will set!"

CHAPTER IX

"LET US GO IN, ALLAN!"

It is very difficult for me to describe the period of time which elapsed

between my arrival at Babyan's Peak and my marriage with Stella. When I

look back on it, it seems sweet as with the odour of flowers, and dim

as with the happy dusk of summer eves, while through the sweetness comes

the sound of Stella's voice, and through the gloom shines the starlight

of her eyes. I think that we loved each other from the first, though for

a while we said no word of love. Day by day I went about the place with

her, accompanied by little Tota and Hendrika only, while she attended

to the thousand and one matters which her father's ever-growing weakness

had laid upon her; or rather, as time drew on, I attended to the

business, and she accompanied me. All day through we were together. Then

after supper, when the night had fallen, we would walk together in the

garden and come at length to hear her father read aloud sometimes from

the works of a poet, sometimes from history. Or, if he did not feel

well, Stella would read, and when this was done, Mr. Carson would

celebrate a short form of prayer, and we would separate till the morning

once more brought our happy hour of meeting.

So the weeks went by, and with every week I grew to know my darling

better. Often, I wonder now, if my fond fancy deceives me, or if indeed

there are women as sweet and dear as she. Was it solitude that had given

such depth and gentleness to her? Was it the long years of communing with Nature that had endowed her with such peculiar grace, the grace we find in opening flowers and budding trees? Had she caught that murmuring voice from the sound of the streams which fall continually about her rocky home? was it the tenderness of the evening sky beneath which she loved to walk, that lay like a shadow on her face, and the light of the evening stars that shone in her quiet eyes? At the least to me she was the realization of that dream which haunts the sleep of sin-stained men; so my memory paints her, so I hope to find her when at last the sleep has rolled away and the fevered dreams are done.

At last there came a day--the most blessed of my life, when we told our love. We had been together all the morning, but after dinner Mr. Carson was so unwell that Stella stopped in with him. At supper we met again, and after supper, when she had put little Tota, to whom she had grown much attached, to bed, we went out, leaving Mr. Carson dozing on the couch.

The night was warm and lovely, and without speaking we walked up the garden to the orange grove and sat down upon a rock. There was a little breeze which shook the petals of the orange blooms over us in showers, and bore their delicate fragrance far and wide. Silence reigned around, broken only by the sound of the falling waterfalls that now died to a faint murmur, and now, as the wavering breeze turned, boomed loudly in our ears. The moon was not yet visible, but already the dark clouds which floated through the sky above us--for there had been rain--showed a glow of silver, telling us that she shone brightly behind the peak.

Stella began to talk in her low, gentle voice, speaking to me of her
life in the wilderness, how she had grown to love it, how her mind had
gone on from idea to idea, and how she pictured the great rushing world
that she had never seen as it was reflected to her from the books which
she had read. It was a curious vision of life that she had: things were
out of proportion to it; it was more like a dream than a reality--a
mirage than the actual face of things. The idea of great cities, and
especially of London, had a kind of fascination for her: she could
scarcely realize the rush, the roar and hurry, the hard crowds of men
and women, strangers to each other, feverishly seeking for wealth and
pleasure beneath a murky sky, and treading one another down in the fury
of their competition.

"What is it all for?" she asked earnestly. "What do they seek? Having so
few years to live, why do they waste them thus?"

I told her that in the majority of instances it was actual hard
necessity that drove them on, but she could barely understand me. Living
as she had done, in the midst of the teeming plenty of a fruitful earth,
she did not seem to be able to grasp the fact that there were millions
who from day to day know not how to stay their hunger.

"I never want to go there," she went on; "I should be bewildered and
frightened to death. It is not natural to live like that. God put Adam
and Eve in a garden, and that is how he meant their children to live--in
peace, and looking always on beautiful things. This is my idea of

128

perfect life. I want no other."

"I thought you once told me that you found it lonely," I said.

"So I did," she answered, innocently, "but that was before you came. Now I am not lonely any more, and it is perfect--perfect as the night."

Just then the full moon rose above the elbow of the peak, and her rays stole far and wide down the misty valley, gleaming on the water, brooding on the plain, searching out the hidden places of the rocks, wrapping the fair form of nature as in a silver bridal veil through which her beauty shone mysteriously.

Stella looked down the terraced valley; she turned and looked up at the scarred face of the golden moon, and then she looked at me. The beauty of the night was about her face, the scent of the night was on her hair, the mystery of the night shone in her shadowed eyes. She looked at me, I looked on her, and all our hearts' love blossomed within us. We spoke no word--we had no words to speak, but slowly we drew near, till lips were pressed to lips as we kissed our eternal troth.

It was she who broke that holy silence, speaking in a changed voice, in soft deep notes that thrilled me like the lowest chords of a smitten harp.

"Ah, now I understand," she said, "now I know why we are lonely, and how we can lose our loneliness. Now I know what it is that stirs us in the beauty of the sky, in the sound of water and in the scent of flowers. It is Love who speaks in everything, though till we hear his voice we understand nothing. But when we hear, then the riddle is answered and the gates of our heart are opened, and, Allan, we see the way that wends through death to heaven, and is lost in the glory of which our love is but a shadow.

"Let us go in, Allan. Let us go before the spell breaks, so that whatever overtakes us, sorrow, death, or separation, we may always have this perfect memory to save us. Come, dearest, let us go!"

I rose like a man in a dream, still holding her by the hand. But as I rose my eye fell upon something that gleamed white among the foliage of the orange bush at my side. I said nothing, but looked. The breeze stirred the orange leaves, the moonlight struck for a moment full upon the white object.

It was the face of Hendrika, the Babyan-woman, as Indaba-zimbi had called her, and on it was a glare of hate that made me shudder.

I said nothing; the face vanished, and just then I heard a baboon bark in the rocks behind.

Then we went down the garden, and Stella passed into the centre hut. I saw Hendrika standing in the shadow near the door, and went up to her.

"Hendrika," I said, "why were you watching Miss Stella and myself in the garden?"

She drew her lips up till her teeth gleamed in the moonlight.

"Have I not watched her these many years, Macumazahn? Shall I cease to watch because a wandering white man comes to steal her? Why were you kissing her in the garden, Macumazahn? How dare you kiss her who is a star?"

"I kissed her because I love her, and because she loves me," I answered. "What has that to do with you, Hendrika?"

"Because you love her," she hissed in answer; "and do I not love her also, who saved me from the babyans? I am a woman as she is, and you are a man, and they say in the kraals that men love women better than women love women. But it is a lie, though this is true, that if a woman loves a man she forgets all other love. Have I not seen it? I gather her flowers--beautiful flowers; I climb the rocks where you would never dare to go to find them; you pluck a piece of orange bloom in the garden and give it to her. What does she do?--she takes the orange bloom, she puts it in her breast, and lets my flowers die. I call to her--she does not hear me--she is thinking. You whisper to some one far away, and she hears and smiles. She used to kiss me sometimes; now she kisses that white brat you brought, because you brought it. Oh, I see it all--all; I

131

have seen it from the first; you are stealing her from us, stealing her to yourself, and those who loved her before you came are forgotten. Be careful, Macumazahn, be careful, lest I am revenged upon you. You, you hate me; you think me half a monkey; that servant of yours calls me Baboon-woman. Well, I have lived with baboons, and they are clever--yes, they can play tricks and know things that you don't, and I am cleverer than they, for I have learnt the wisdom of white people also, and I say to you, Walk softly, Macumazahn, or you will fall into a pit," and with one more look of malice she was gone.

I stood for a moment reflecting. I was afraid of this strange creature who seemed to combine the cunning of the great apes that had reared her with the passions and skill of human kind. I foreboded evil at her hands. And yet there was something almost touching in the fierceness of her jealousy. It is generally supposed that this passion only exists in strength when the object loved is of another sex from the lover, but I confess that, both in this instance and in some others which I have met with, this has not been my experience. I have known men, and especially uncivilized men, who were as jealous of the affection of their friend or master as any lover could be of that of his mistress; and who has not seen cases of the same thing where parents and their children are concerned? But the lower one gets in the scale of humanity, the more readily this passion thrives; indeed, it may be said to come to its intensest perfection in brutes. Women are more jealous than men, small-hearted men are more jealous than those of larger mind and wider sympathy, and animals are the most jealous of all. Now Hendrika was in some ways not far removed from animal, which may perhaps account for the ferocity of her jealousy of her mistress's affection.

Shaking off my presentiments of evil, I entered the centre hut. Mr. Carson was resting on the sofa, and by him knelt Stella holding his hand, and her head resting on his breast. I saw at once that she had been telling him of what had come about between us; nor was I sorry, for it is a task that a would-be son-in-law is generally glad to do by deputy.

"Come here, Allan Quatermain," he said, almost sternly, and my heart gave a jump, for I feared lest he might be about to require me to go about my business. But I came.

"Stella tells me," he went on, "that you two have entered into a marriage engagement. She tells me also that she loves you, and that you say that you love her."

"I do indeed, sir," I broke in; "I love her truly; if ever a woman was loved in this world, I love her."

"I thank Heaven for it," said the old man. "Listen, my children. Many years ago a great shame and sorrow fell upon me, so great a sorrow that, as I sometimes think, it affected my brain. At any rate, I determined to do what most men would have considered the act of a madman, to go far away into the wilderness with my only child, there to live remote from

civilization and its evils. I did so; I found this place, and here we
have lived for many years, happily enough, and perhaps not without doing
good in our generation, but still in a way unnatural to our race and
status. At first I thought I would let my daughter grow up in a state of
complete ignorance, that she should be Nature's child. But as time went
on, I saw the folly and the wickedness of my plan. I had no right to
degrade her to the level of the savages around me, for if the fruit
of the tree of knowledge is a bitter fruit, still it teaches good from
evil. So I educated her as well as I was able, till in the end I knew
that in mind, as in body, she was in no way inferior to her sisters, the
children of the civilized world. She grew up and entered into womanhood,
and then it came into my mind that I was doing her a bitter wrong, that
I was separating her from her kind and keeping her in a wilderness where
she could find neither mate nor companion. But though I knew this, I
could not yet make up my mind to return to active life; I had grown to
love this place. I dreaded to return into the world I had abjured. Again
and again I put my resolutions aside. Then at the commencement of this
year I fell ill. For a while I waited, hoping that I might get better,
but at last I realized that I should never get better, that the hand of
Death was upon me."

"Ah, no, father, not that!" Stella said, with a cry.

"Yes, love, that, and it is true. Now you will be able to forget our
separation in the happiness of a new meeting," and he glanced at me
and smiled. "Well, when this knowledge came home to me, I determined to

abandon this place and trek for the coast, though I well knew that
the journey would kill me. I should never live to reach it. But Stella
would, and it would be better than leaving her here alone with savages
in the wilderness. On the very day that I had made up my mind to take
this step Stella found you dying in the Bad Lands, Allan Quatermain, and
brought you here. She brought you, of all men in the world, you, whose
father had been my dear friend, and who once with your baby hands had
saved her life from fire, that she might live to save yours from thirst.
At the time I said little, but I saw the hand of Providence in this, and
I determined to wait and see what came about between you. At the worst,
if nothing came about, I soon learned that I could trust you to see her
safely to the coast after I was gone. But many days ago I knew how it
stood between you, and now things are determined as I prayed they might
be. God bless you both, my children; may you be happy in your love;
may it endure till death and beyond it. God bless you both!" and he
stretched out his hand towards me.

I took it, and Stella kissed him.

Presently he spoke again--

"It is my intention," he said, "if you two consent, to marry you next
Sunday. I wish to do so soon, for I do not know how much longer will be
allowed to me. I believe that such a ceremony, solemnly celebrated
and entered into before witnesses, will, under the circumstances, be
perfectly legal; but of course you will repeat it with every formality

135

the first moment it lies in your power so to do. And now, there is
one more thing: when I left England my fortunes were in a shattered
condition; in the course of years they have recovered themselves,
the accumulated rents, as I heard but recently, when the waggons last
returned from Port Natal, have sufficed to pay off all charges, and
there is a considerable balance over. Consequently you will not marry on
nothing, for of course you, Stella, are my heiress, and I wish to make
a stipulation. It is this. That so soon as my death occurs you should
leave this place and take the first opportunity of returning to England.
I do not ask you to live there always; it might prove too much for
people reared in the wilds, as both of you have been; but I do ask you
to make it your permanent home. Do you consent and promise this?"

"I do," I answered.

"And so do I," said Stella.

"Very well," he answered; "and now I am tired out. Again God bless you
both, and good-night."

CHAPTER X

HENDRIKA PLOTS EVIL

On the following morning I had a conversation with Indaba-zimbi. First
of all I told him that I was going to marry Stella.

"Oh!" he said, "I thought so, Macumazahn. Did I not tell you that you
would find happiness on this journey? Most men must be content to watch
the Star from a long way off, to you it is given to wear her on your
heart. But remember, Macumazahn, remember that stars set."

"Can you not stop your croaking even for a day?" I answered, angrily,
for his words sent a thrill of fear through me.

"A true prophet must tell the ill as well as the good, Macumazahn. I
only speak what is on my mind. But what of it? What is life but loss,
loss upon loss, till life itself be lost? But in death we may find all
the things that we have lost. So your father taught, Macumazahn, and
there was wisdom in his gentleness. Ou! I do not believe in death; it is
change, that is all, Macumazahn. Look now, the rain falls, the drops of
rain that were one water in the clouds fall side by side. They sink into
the ground; presently the sun will come out, the earth will be dry, the
drops will be gone. A fool looks and says the drops are dead, they will
never be one again, they will never again fall side by side. But I am a
rain-maker, and I know the ways of rain. It is not true. The drops will

drain by many paths into the river, and will be one water there. They will go up to the clouds again in the mists of morning, and there will again be as they have been. We are the drops of rain, Macumazahn. When we fall that is our life. When we sink into the ground that is death, and when we are drawn up again to the sky, what is that, Macumazahn? No! no! when we find we lose, and when we seem to lose, then we shall really find. I am not a Christian, Macumazahn, but I am old, and have watched and seen things that perhaps Christians do not see. There, I have spoken. Be happy with your star, and if it sets, wait, Macumazahn, wait till it rises again. It will not be long; one day you will go to sleep, then your eyes will open on another sky, and there your star will be shining, Macumazahn."

I made no answer at the time. I could not bear to talk of such a thing. But often and often in the after years I have thought of Indaba-zimbi and his beautiful simile and gathered comfort from it. He was a strange man, this old rain-making savage, and there was more wisdom in him than in many learned atheists--those spiritual destroyers who, in the name of progress and humanity, would divorce hope from life, and leave us wandering in a lonesome, self-consecrated hell.

"Indaba-zimbi," I said, changing the subject, "I have something to say," and I told him of the threats of Hendrika.

He listened with an unmoved face, nodding his white lock at intervals as the narrative went on. But I saw that he was disturbed by it.

"Macumazahn," he said at length, "I have told you that this is an evil woman. She was nourished on baboon milk, and the baboon nature is in her veins. Such creatures should be killed, not kept. She will make you mischief if she can. But I will watch her, Macumazahn. Look, the Star is waiting for you; go, or she will hate me as Hendrika hates you."

So I went, nothing loth, for attractive as was the wisdom of Indaba-zimbi, I found a deeper meaning in Stella's simplest word. All the rest of that day I passed in her company, and the greater part of the two following days. At last came Saturday night, the eve of our marriage. It rained that night, so we did not go out, but spent the evening in the hut. We sat hand in hand, saying little, but Mr. Carson talked a good deal, telling us tales of his youth, and of countries that he had visited. Then he read aloud from the Bible, and bade us goodnight. I also kissed Stella and went to bed. I reached my hut by the covered way, and before I undressed opened the door to see what the night was like. It was very dark, and rain was still falling, but as the light streamed out into the gloom I fancied that I caught sight of a dusky form gliding away. The thought of Hendrika flashed into my mind; could she be skulking about outside there? Now I had said nothing of Hendrika and her threats either to Mr. Carson or Stella, because I did not wish to alarm them. Also I knew that Stella was attached to this strange person, and I did not wish to shake her confidence in her unless it was absolutely necessary. For a minute or two I stood hesitating, then, reflecting that if it was Hendrika, there she should stop, I went in and put up the stout wooden bar that was used to secure the door. For the last few nights old Indaba-zimbi had made a habit of sleeping in the covered passage, which was the only other possible way of access. As I came to bed I had stepped over him rolled up in his blanket, and to all appearances fast asleep. So it being evident that I had nothing to fear, I promptly dismissed the matter from my mind, which, as may be imagined, was indeed fully occupied with other thoughts.

I got into bed, and for awhile lay awake thinking of the great happiness in store for me, and of the providential course of events that had brought it within my reach. A few weeks since and I was wandering in the desert a dying man, bearing a dying child, and with scarcely a possession left in the world except a store of buried ivory that I never expected to see again. And now I was about to wed one of the sweetest and loveliest women on the whole earth--a woman whom I loved more than I could have thought possible, and who loved me back again. Also, as though that were not good fortune enough, I was to acquire with her very considerable possessions, quite sufficiently large to enable us to follow any plan of life we found agreeable. As I lay and reflected on all this I grew afraid of my good fortune. Old Indaba-zimbi's melancholy prophecies came into my mind. Hitherto he had always prophesied truly. What if these should be true also? I turned cold as I thought of it, and prayed to the Power above to preserve us both to live and love together. Never was prayer more needed. While its words were still upon my lips I dropped asleep and dreamed a most dreadful dream.

I dreamed that Stella and I were standing together to be married. She was dressed in white, and radiant with beauty, but it was a wild, spiritual beauty which frightened me. Her eyes shone like stars, a pale flame played about her features, and the wind that blew did not stir her hair. Nor was this all, for her white robes were death wrappings, and the altar at which we stood was formed of the piled-up earth from an open grave that yawned between us. So we stood waiting for one to wed us, but no one came. Presently from the open grave sprang the form of Hendrika. In her hand was a knife, with which she stabbed at me, but pierced the heart of Stella, who, without a cry, fell backwards into the grave, still looking at me as she fell. Then Hendrika leaped after her into the grave. I heard her feet strike heavily.

"Awake, Macumazahn! awake!" cried the voice of Indaba-zimbi.

I awoke and bounded from the bed, a cold perspiration pouring from me. In the darkness on the other side of the hut I heard sounds of furious struggling. Luckily I kept my head. Just by me was a chair on which were matches and a rush taper. I struck a match and held it to the taper. Now in the growing light I could see two forms rolling one over the other on the floor, and from between them came the flash of steel. The fat melted and the light burnt up. It was Indaba-zimbi and the woman Hendrika who were struggling, and, what is more, the woman was getting the better of the man, strong as he was. I rushed towards them. Now she was uppermost, now she had wrenched herself from his fierce grip, and now the great knife she had in her hand flashed up.

141

But I was behind her, and, placing my hands beneath her arms, jerked with all my strength. She fell backwards, and, in her effort to save herself, most fortunately dropped the knife. Then we flung ourselves upon her. Heavens! the strength of that she-devil! Nobody who has not experienced it could believe it. She fought and scratched and bit, and at one time nearly mastered the two of us. As it was she did break loose. She rushed at the bed, sprung on it, and bounded thence straight up at the roof of the hut. I never saw such a jump, and could not conceive what she meant to do. In the roof were the peculiar holes which I have described. They were designed to admit light, and covered with overhanging eaves. She sprung straight and true like a monkey, and, catching the edge of the hole with her hands, strove to draw herself through it. But here her strength, exhausted with the long struggle, failed her. For a moment she swung, then dropped to the ground and fell senseless.

"Ou!" gasped Indaba-zimbi. "Let us tie the devil up before she comes to life again."

I thought this a good counsel, so we took a reim that lay in the corner of the room, and lashed her hands and feet in such a fashion that even she could scarcely escape. Then we carried her into the passage, and Indaba-zimbi sat over her, the knife in his hand, for I did not wish to raise an alarm at that hour of the night.

"Do you know how I caught her, Macumazahn?" he said. "For several nights I have slept here with one eye open, for I thought she had made a plan. To-night I kept wide awake, though I pretended to be asleep. An hour after you got into the blankets the moon rose, and I saw a beam of light come into the hut through the hole in the roof. Presently I saw the beam of light vanish. At first I thought that a cloud was passing over the moon, but I listened and heard a noise as though some one was squeezing himself through a narrow space. Presently he was through, and hanging by his hands. Then the light came in again, and in the middle of it I saw the Babyan-frau swinging from the roof, and about to drop into the hut. She clung by both hands, and in her mouth was a great knife. She dropped, and I ran forward to seize her as she dropped, and gripped her round the middle. But she heard me come, and, seizing the knife, struck at me in the dark and missed me. Then we struggled, and you know the rest. You were very nearly dead to-night, Macumazahn."

"Very nearly indeed," I answered, still panting, and arranging the rags of my night-dress round me as best I might. Then the memory of my horrid dream flashed into my mind. Doubtless it had been conjured up by the sound of Hendrika dropping to the floor--in my dream it had been a grave that she dropped into. All of it, then, had been experienced in that second of time. Well, dreams are swift; perhaps Time itself is nothing but a dream, and events that seem far apart really occur simultaneously.

We passed the rest of the night watching Hendrika. Presently she came to herself and struggled furiously to break the reim. But the untanned buffalo hide was too strong even for her, and, moreover, Indaba-zimbi unceremoniously sat upon her to keep her quiet. At last she gave it up.

In due course the day broke--my marriage day. Leaving Indaba-zimbi to watch my would-be murderess, I went and fetched some natives from the stables, and with their aid bore Hendrika to the prison hut--that same hut in which she had been confined when she had been brought a baboon-child from the rocks. Here we shut her up, and, leaving Indaba-zimbi to watch outside, I returned to my sleeping-place and dressed in the best garments that the Babyan Kraals could furnish. But when I looked at the reflection of my face, I was horrified. It was covered with scratches inflicted by the nails of Hendrika. I doctored them up as best I could, then went out for a walk to calm my nerves, which, what between the events of the past night, and of those pending that day, were not a little disturbed.

When I returned it was breakfast time. I went into the dining hut, and there Stella was waiting to greet me, dressed in simple white and with orange flowers on her breast. She came forward to me shyly enough; then, seeing the condition of my face, started back.

"Why, Allan! what have you been doing to yourself?" she asked.

As I was about to answer, her father came in leaning on his stick, and, catching sight of me, instantly asked the same question.

144

Then I told them everything, both of Hendrika's threats and of her fierce attempt to carry them into execution. But I did not tell my horrid dream.

Stella's face grew white as the flowers on her breast, but that of her father became very stern.

"You should have spoken of this before, Allan," he said. "I now see that I did wrong to attempt to civilize this wicked and revengeful creature, who, if she is human, has all the evil passions of the brutes that reared her. Well, I will make an end of it this very day."

"Oh, father," said Stella, "don't have her killed. It is all dreadful enough, but that would be more dreadful still. I have been very fond of her, and, bad as she is, she has loved me. Do not have her killed on my marriage day."

"No," her father answered, "she shall not be killed, for though she deserves to die, I will not have her blood upon our hands. She is a brute, and has followed the nature of brutes. She shall go back whence she came."

No more was said on the matter at the time, but when breakfast--which was rather a farce--was done, Mr. Carson sent for his headman and gave him certain orders.

145

We were to be married after the service which Mr. Carson held every Sunday morning in the large marble hut set apart for that purpose. The service began at ten o'clock, but long before that hour all the natives on the place came up in troops, singing as they came, to be present at the wedding of the "Star." It was a pretty sight to see them, the men dressed in all their finery, and carrying shields and sticks in their hands, and the women and children bearing green branches of trees, ferns, and flowers. At length, about half-past nine, Stella rose, pressed my hand, and left me to my reflections. A few minutes to ten she reappeared again with her father, dressed in a white veil, a wreath of orange flowers on her dark curling hair, a bouquet of orange flowers in her hand. To me she seemed like a dream of loveliness. With her came little Tota in a high state of glee and excitement. She was Stella's only bridesmaid. Then we all passed out towards the church hut. The bare space in front of it was filled with hundreds of natives, who set up a song as we came. But we went on into the hut, which was crowded with such of the natives as usually worshipped there. Here Mr. Carson, as usual, read the service, though he was obliged to sit down in order to do so. When it was done--and to me it seemed interminable--Mr. Carson whispered that he meant to marry us outside the hut in sight of all the people. So we went out and took our stand under the shade of a large tree that grew near the hut facing the bare space where the natives were gathered.

Mr. Carson held up his hand to enjoin silence. Then, speaking in the native dialect, he told them that he was about to make us man and wife

146

after the Christian fashion and in the sight of all men. This done, he proceeded to read the marriage service over us, and very solemnly and beautifully he did it. We said the words, I placed the ring--it was her father's signet ring, for we had no other--upon Stella's finger, and it was done.

Then Mr. Carson spoke. "Allan and Stella," he said, "I believe that the ceremony which has been performed makes you man and wife in the sight of God and man, for all that is necessary to make a marriage binding is, that it should be celebrated according to the custom of the country where the parties to it reside. It is according to the custom that has been in force here for fifteen years or more that you have been married in the face of all the people, and in token of it you will both sign the register that I have kept of such marriages, among those of my people who have adopted the Christian Faith. Still, in case there should be any legal flaw I again demand the solemn promise of you both that on the first opportunity you will cause this marriage to be re-celebrated in some civilized land. Do you promise?"

"We do," we answered.

Then the book was brought out and we signed our names. At first my wife signed hers "Stella" only, but her father bade her write it Stella Carson for the first and last time in her life. Then several of the indunas, or headmen, including old Indaba-zimbi, put their marks in witness. Indaba-zimbi drew his mark in the shape of a little star, in humorous allusion to Stella's native name. That register is before me now as I write. That, with a lock of my darling's hair which lies between its leaves, is my dearest possession. There are all the names and marks as they were written many years ago beneath the shadow of the tree at Babyan Kraals in the wilderness, but alas! and alas! where are those who wrote them?

"My people," said Mr. Carson, when the signing was done, and we had kissed each other before them all--"My people, Macumazahn and the Star, my daughter, are now man and wife, to live in one kraal, to eat of one bowl, to share one fortune till they reach the grave. Hear now, my people, you know this woman," and turning he pointed to Hendrika, who, unseen by us, had been led out of the prison hut.

"Yes, yes, we know her," said a little ring of headmen, who formed the primitive court of justice, and after the fashion of natives had squatted themselves in a circle on the ground in front of us. "We know her, she is the white Babyan-woman, she is Hendrika, the body servant of the Star."

"You know her," said Mr. Carson, "but you do not know her altogether. Stand forward, Indaba-zimbi, and tell the people what came about last night in the hut of Macumazahn."

Accordingly old Indaba-zimbi came forward, and, squatting down, told his moving tale with much descriptive force and many gestures, finishing up by producing the great knife from which his watchfulness had saved me.

Then I was called upon, and in a few brief words substantiated his story: indeed my face did that in the sight of all men.

Then Mr. Carson turned to Hendrika, who stood in sullen silence, her eyes fixed upon the ground, and asked her if she had anything to say.

She looked up boldly and answered--

"Macumazahn has robbed me of the love of my mistress. I would have robbed him of his life, which is a little thing compared to that which I have lost at his hands. I have failed, and I am sorry for it, for had I killed him and left no trace the Star would have forgotten him and shone on me again."

"Never," murmured Stella in my ear; but Mr. Carson turned white with wrath.

"My people," he said, "you hear the words of this woman. You hear how she pays me back, me and my daughter whom she swears she loves. She says that she would have murdered a man who has done her no evil, the man who is the husband of her mistress. We saved her from the babyans, we tamed her, we fed her, we taught her, and this is how she pays us back. Say, my people, what reward should be given to her?"

"Death," said the circle of indunas, pointing their thumbs downwards, and all the multitude beyond echoed the word "Death."

"Death," repeated the head induna, adding, "If you save her, my father, we will slay her with our own hands. She is a Babyan-woman, a devil-woman; ah, yes, we have heard of such before; let her be slain before she works more evil."

Then it was that Stella stepped forward and begged for Hendrika's life in moving terms. She pleaded the savagery of the woman's nature, her long service, and the affection that she had always shown towards herself. She said that I, whose life had been attempted, forgave her, and she, my wife, who had nearly been left a widow before she was made a bride, forgave her; let them forgive her also, let her be sent away, not slain, let not her marriage day be stained with blood.

Now her father listened readily enough, for he had no intention of killing Hendrika--indeed, he had already promised not to do so. But the people were in a different humour, they looked upon Hendrika as a devil, and would have torn her to pieces there and then, could they have had their way. Nor were matters mended by Indaba-zimbi, who had already gained a great reputation for wisdom and magic in the place. Suddenly the old man rose and made quite an impassioned speech, urging them to kill Hendrika at once or mischief would come of it.

At last matters got very bad, for two of the Indunas came forward to

drag her off to execution, and it was not until Stella burst into tears
that the sight of her grief, backed by Mr. Carson's orders and my own
remonstrances, carried the day.

All this while Hendrika had been standing quite unmoved. At last the
tumult ceased, and the leading induna called to her to go, promising
that if ever she showed her face near the kraals again she should be
stabbed like a jackal. Then Hendrika spoke to Stella in a low voice and
in English--

"Better let them kill me, mistress, better for all. Without you to love
I shall go mad and become a babyan again."

Stella did not answer, and they loosed her. She stepped forward and
looked at the natives with a stare of hate. Then she turned and walked
past me, and as she passed whispered a native phrase in my ear, that,
being literally translated, means, "Till another moon," but which has
the same significance as the French "au revoir."

It frightened me, for I knew she meant that she had not done with me,
and saw that our mercy was misplaced. Seeing my face change she ran
swiftly from me, and as she passed Indaba-zimbi, with a sudden movement
snatched her great knife from his hand. When she had gone about twenty
paces she halted, looked long and earnestly on Stella, gave one loud cry
of anguish, and fled. A few minutes later we saw her far away, bounding
up the face of an almost perpendicular cliff--a cliff that nobody except

herself and the baboons could possibly climb.

"Look," said Indaba-zimbi in my ear--"Look, Macumazahn, there goes the
Babyan-frau. But, Macumazahn, she will come back again. Ah, why
will you not listen to my words. Have they not always been true words,
Macumazahn?" and he shrugged his shoulders and turned away.

For a while I was much disturbed, but at any rate Hendrika was gone for
the present, and Stella, my dear and lovely wife, was there at my side,
and in her smiles I forgot my fears.

For the rest of that day, why should I write of it?--there are things
too happy and too sacred to be written of.

At last I had, if only for a little while, found that rest, that perfect
joy which we seek so continually and so rarely clasp.

CHAPTER XI

GONE!

I wonder if many married couples are quite as happy as we found ourselves. Cynics, a growing class, declare that few illusions can survive a honeymoon. Well, I do not know about it, for I only married once, and can but speak from my limited experience. But certainly our illusion, or rather the great truth of which it is the shadow, did survive, as to this day it survives in my heart across all the years of utter separation, and across the unanswering gulf of gloom.

But complete happiness is not allowed in this world even for an hour. As our marriage day had been shadowed by the scene which has been described, so our married life was shadowed by its own sorrow.

Three days after our wedding Mr. Carson had a stroke. It had been long impending, now it fell. We came into the centre hut to dinner and found him lying speechless on the couch. At first I thought that he was dying, but this was not so. On the contrary, within four days he recovered his speech and some power of movement. But he never recovered his memory, though he still knew Stella, and sometimes myself. Curiously enough he remembered little Tota best of all three, though occasionally he thought that she was his own daughter in her childhood, and would ask her where her mother was. This state of affairs lasted for some seven months. The old man gradually grew weaker, but he did not die. Of course his condition quite precluded the idea of our leaving Babyan Kraals till all was over. This was the more distressing to me because I had a nervous presentiment that Stella was incurring danger by staying there, and also because the state of her health rendered it desirable that we should reach a civilized region as soon as possible. However, it could not be helped.

At length the end came very suddenly. We were sitting one evening by Mr. Carson's bedside in his hut, when to our astonishment he sat up and spoke in a strong, full voice.

"I hear you," he said. "Yes, yes, I forgive you. Poor woman! you too have suffered," and he fell back dead.

I have little doubt that he was addressing his lost wife, some vision of whom had flashed across his dying sense. Stella, of course, was overwhelmed with grief at her loss. Till I came her father had been her sole companion, and therefore, as may be imagined, the tie between them was much closer than is usual even in the case of father and daughter. So deeply did she mourn that I began to fear for the effect upon her health. Nor were we the only ones to grieve; all the natives on the settlement called Mr. Carson "father," and as a father they lamented him. The air resounded with the wailing of women, and the men went about with bowed heads, saying that "the sun had set in the heavens, now only the Star (Stella) remained." Indaba-zimbi alone did not mourn. He said that it was best that the Inkoos should die, for what was life worth when one lay like a log?--moreover, that it would have been well for all if he had died sooner.

On the following day we buried him in the little graveyard near the waterfall. It was a sad business, and Stella cried very much, in spite of all I could do to comfort her.

That night as I sat outside the hut smoking--for the weather was hot, and Stella was lying down inside--old Indaba-zimbi came up, saluted, and squatted at my feet.

"What is it, Indaba-zimbi?" I said.

"This, Macumazahn. When are you going to trek towards the coast?"

"I don't know," I answered. "The Star is not fit to travel now, we must wait awhile."

"No, Macumazahn, you must not wait, you must go, and the Star must take her chance. She is strong. It is nothing. All will be well."

"Why do you say so? why must we go?"

"For this reason, Macumazahn," and he looked cautiously round and spoke low. "The baboons have come back in thousands. All the mountain is full

155

of them."

"I did not know that they had gone," I said.

"Yes," he answered, "they went after the marriage, all but one or two; now they are back, all the baboons in the world, I think. I saw a whole cliff back with them."

"Is that all?" I said, for I saw that he had something behind. "I am not afraid of a pack of baboons."

"No, Macumazahn, it is not all. The Babyan-frau, Hendrika, is with them."

Now nothing had been heard or seen of Hendrika since her expulsion, and though at first she and her threats had haunted me somewhat, by degrees she to a great extent had passed out of my mind, which was fully preoccupied with Stella and my father-in-law's illness. I started violently. "How do you know this?" I asked.

"I know it because I saw her, Macumazahn. She is disguised, she is dressed up in baboon skins, and her face is stained dark. But though she was a long way off, I knew her by her size, and I saw the white flesh of her arm when the skins slipped aside. She has come back, Macumazahn, with all the baboons in the world, and she has come back to do evil. Now do you understand why you should trek?"

"Yes," I said, "though I don't see how she and the baboons can harm us, I think that it will be better to go. If necessary we can camp the waggons somewhere for a while on the journey. Hearken, Indaba-zimbi: say nothing of this to the Star; I will not have her frightened. And hearken again. Speak to the headmen, and see that watchers are set all round the huts and gardens, and kept there night and day. To-morrow we will get the waggons ready, and next day we will trek."

He nodded his white lock and went to do my bidding, leaving me not a little disturbed--unreasonably so, indeed. It was a strange story. That this woman had the power of conversing with baboons I knew.[*] That was not so very wonderful, seeing that the Bushmen claim to be able to do the same thing, and she had been nurtured by them. But that she had been able to muster them, and by the strength of her human will and intelligence muster them in order to forward her ends of revenge, seemed to me so incredible that after reflection my fears grew light. Still I determined to trek. After all, a journey in an ox waggon would not be such a very terrible thing to a strong woman accustomed to roughing it, whatever her state of health. And when all was said and done I did not like this tale of the presence of Hendrika with countless hosts of baboons.

[*] For an instance of this, see Anderson's "Twenty-five Years in a Waggon," vol. i. p. 262.--Editor.

So I went in to Stella, and without saying a word to her of the baboon story, told her I had been thinking matters over, and had come to the conclusion that it was our duty to follow her father's instructions to the letter, and leave Babyan Kraals at once. Into all our talk I need not enter, but the end of it was that she agreed with me, and declared that she could quite well manage the journey, saying, moreover, that now that her dear father was dead she would be glad to get away.

Nothing happened to disturb us that night, and on the following morning I was up early making preparations. The despair of the people when they learned that we were going to leave them was something quite pitiable. I could only console them by declaring that we were but on a journey, and would return the following year.

"They had lived in the shadow of their father, who was dead," they declared; "ever since they were little they had lived in his shadow. He had received them when they were outcasts and wanderers without a mat to lie on, or a blanket to cover them, and they had grown fat in his shadow. Then he had died, and the Star, their father's daughter, had married me, Macumazahn, and they had believed that I should take their father's place, and let them live in my shadow. What should they do when there was no one to protect them? The tribes were kept from attacking them by fear of the white man. If we went they would be eaten up," and so on. Alas! there was but too much foundation for their fears.

I returned to the huts at mid-day to get some dinner. Stella said that she was going to pack during the afternoon, so I did not think it necessary to caution her about going out alone, as I did not wish to allude to the subject of Hendrika and the baboons unless I was obliged to. I told her, however, that I would come back to help her as soon as I could get away. Then I went down to the native kraals to sort out such cattle as had belonged to Mr. Carson from those which belonged to the Kaffirs, for I proposed to take them with us. It was a large herd, and the business took an incalculable time. At length, a little before sundown, I gave it up, and leaving Indaba-zimbi to finish the job, got on my horse and rode homewards.

Arriving, I gave the horse to one of the stable boys, and went into the central hut. There was no sign of Stella, though the things she had been packing lay about the floor. I passed first into our sleeping hut, thence one by one into all the others, but still saw no sign of her. Then I went out, and calling to a Kaffir in the garden asked him if he had seen his mistress.

He answered "yes." He had seen her carrying flowers and walking towards the graveyard, holding the little white girl--my daughter--as he called her, by the hand, when the sun stood "there," and he pointed to a spot on the horizon where it would have been about an hour and a half before. "The two dogs were with them," he added. I turned and ran towards the graveyard, which was about a quarter of a mile from the huts. Of course there was no reason to be anxious--evidently she had gone to lay the flowers on her father's grave. And yet I was anxious.

159

When I got near the graveyard I met one of the natives, who, by my orders, had been set round the kraals to watch the place, and noticed that he was rubbing his eyes and yawning. Clearly he had been asleep. I asked him if he had seen his mistress, and he answered that he had not, which under the circumstances was not wonderful. Without stopping to reproach him, I ordered the man to follow me, and went on to the graveyard. There, on Mr. Carson's grave, lay the drooping flowers which Stella had been carrying, and there in the fresh mould was the spoor of Tota's veldschoon, or hide slipper. But where were they?

I ran from the graveyard and called aloud at the top of my voice, but no answer came. Meanwhile the native was more profitably engaged in tracing their spoor. He followed it for about a hundred yards till he came to a clump of mimosa bush that was situated between the stream and the ancient marble quarries just over the waterfall, and at the mouth of the ravine. Here he stopped, and I heard him give a startled cry. I rushed to the spot, passed through the trees, and saw this. The little open space in the centre of the glade had been the scene of a struggle. There, in the soft earth, were the marks of three pairs of human feet--two shod, one naked--Stella's, Tota's, and Hendrika's. Nor was this all. There, close by, lay the fragments of the two dogs--they were nothing more--and one baboon, not yet quite dead, which had been bitten in the throat by the dogs. All round was the spoor of numberless baboons. The full horror of what had happened flashed into my mind.

My wife and Tota had been carried off by the baboons. As yet they had
not been killed, for if so their remains would have been found with
those of the dogs. They had been carried off. The brutes, acting under
the direction of that woman-monkey, Hendrika, had dragged them away to
some secret den, there to keep them till they died--or kill them!

For a moment I literally staggered beneath the terror of the shock. Then
I roused myself from my despair. I bade the native run and alarm the
people at the kraals, telling them to come armed, and bring me guns and
ammunition. He went like the wind, and I turned to follow the spoor. For
a few yards it was plain enough--Stella had been dragged along. I could
see where her heels had struck the ground; the child had, I presumed,
been carried--at least there were no marks of her feet. At the water's
edge the spoor vanished. The water was shallow, and they had gone along
in it, or at least Hendrika and her victim had, in order to obliterate
the trail. I could see where a moss-grown stone had been freshly turned
over in the water-bed. I ran along the bank some way up the ravine, in
the vain hope of catching a sight of them. Presently I heard a bark in
the cliffs above me; it was answered by another, and then I saw that
scores of baboons were hidden about among the rocks on either side, and
were softly swinging themselves down to bar the path. To go on unarmed
as I was would be useless. I should only be torn to pieces as the dogs
had been. So I turned and fled back towards the huts. As I drew near I
could see that my messenger had roused the settlement, for natives with
spears and kerries in their hands were running up towards the kraals.
When I reached the hut I met old Indaba-zimbi, who wore a very serious

face.

"So the evil has fallen, Macumazahn," he said.

"It has fallen," I answered.

"Keep a good heart, Macumazahn," he said again. "She is not dead, nor is the little maid, and before they die we shall find them. Remember this, Hendrika loves her. She will not harm her, or allow the babyans to harm her. She will try to hide her away from you, that is all."

"Pray God that we may find her," I groaned. "The light is going fast."

"The moon rises in three hours," he answered; "we will search by moonlight. It is useless to start now; see, the sun sinks. Let us get the men together, eat, and make things ready. Hamba gachla. Hasten slowly, Macumazahn."

As there was no help, I took his advice. I could eat no food, but I packed some up to take with us, and made ready ropes, and a rough kind of litter. If we found them they would scarcely be able to walk. Ah! if we found them! How slowly the time passed! It seemed hours before the moon rose. But at last it did rise.

Then we started. In all we were about a hundred men, but we only mustered five guns between us, my elephant roer and four that had

162

belonged to Mr. Carson.

CHAPTER XII

THE MAGIC OF INDABA-ZIMBI

We gained the spot by the stream where Stella had been taken. The
natives looked at the torn fragments of the dogs, and at the marks of
violence, and I heard them swearing to each other, that whether the
Star lived or died they would not rest till they had exterminated every
baboon on Babyan's Peak. I echoed the oath, and, as shall be seen, we
kept it.

We started on along the stream, following the spoor of the baboons as we
best could. But the stream left no spoor, and the hard, rocky banks very
little. Still we wandered on. All night we wandered through the lonely
moonlit valleys, startling the silence into a thousand echoes with our
cries. But no answer came to them. In vain our eyes searched the sides
of precipices formed of water-riven rocks fantastically piled one
upon another; in vain we searched through endless dells and fern-clad
crannies. There was nothing to be found. How could we expect to find
two human beings hidden away in the recesses of this vast stretch of
mountain ground, which no man yet had ever fully explored. They were
lost, and in all human probability lost for ever.

To and fro we wandered hopelessly, till at last dawn found us footsore
and weary nearly at the spot whence we had started. We sat down waiting
for the sun to rise, and the men ate of such food as they had brought

with them, and sent to the kraals for more.

I sat upon a stone with a breaking heart. I cannot describe my feelings. Let the reader put himself in my position and perhaps he may get some idea of them. Near me was old Indaba-zimbi, who sat staring straight before him as though he were looking into space, and taking note of what went on there. An idea struck me. This man had some occult power. Several times during our adventures he had prophesied, and in every case his prophecies had proved true. He it was who, when we escaped from the Zulu Impi, had told me to steer north, because there we should find the place of a white man who lived under the shadow of a great peak that was full of baboons. Perhaps he could help in this extremity--at any rate it was worth trying.

"Indaba-zimbi," I said, "you say that you can send your spirit through the doors of space and see what we cannot see. At the least I know that you can do strange things. Can you not help me now? If you can, and will save her, I will give you half the cattle that we have here."

"I never said anything of the sort, Macumazahn," he answered. "I do things, I do not talk about them. Neither do I seek reward for what I do like a common witch-doctor. It is well that you have asked me to use my wisdom, Macumazahn, for I should not have used it again without being asked--no, not even for the sake of the Star and yourself, whom I love, for if so my Spirit would have been angry. In the other matters I had a part, for my life was concerned as well as yours; but in this matter I have no part, and therefore I might not use my wisdom unless you thought well to call upon my Spirit. However, it would have been no good to ask me before, for I have only just found the herb I want," and he produced a handful of the leaves of a plant that was unfamiliar to me. It had prickly leaves, shaped very much like those of the common English nettle.

"Now, Macumazahn," he went on, "bid the men leave us alone, and then follow me presently to the little glade down there by the water."

I did so. When I reached the glade I found Indaba-zimbi kindling a small fire under the shadow of a tree by the edge of the water.

"Sit there, Macumazahn," he said, pointing to a stone near the fire, "and do not be surprised or frightened at anything you see. If you move or call out we shall learn nothing."

I sat down and watched. When the fire was alight and burning brightly, the old fellow stripped himself stark naked, and, going to the foot of the pool, dipped himself in the water. Then he came back shivering with the cold, and, leaning over the little fire, thrust leaves of the plant I have mentioned into his mouth and began to chew them, muttering as he chewed. Most of the remaining leaves he threw on to the fire. A dense smoke rose from them, but he held his head in this smoke and drew it down his lungs till I saw that he was exhibiting every sign of suffocation. The veins in his throat and chest swelled, he gasped

166

loudly, and his eyes, from which tears were streaming, seemed as though they were going to start from his head. Presently he fell over on his side, and lay senseless. I was terribly alarmed, and my first impulse was to run to his assistance, but fortunately I remembered his caution, and sat quiet.

Indaba-zimbi lay on the ground like a person quite dead. His limbs had all the utter relaxation of death. But as I watched I saw them begin to stiffen, exactly as though rigor mortis had set in. Then, to my astonishment, I perceived them once more relax, and this time there appeared upon his chest the stain of decomposition. It spread and spread; in three minutes the man, to all appearance, was a livid corpse.

I sat amazed watching this uncanny sight, and wondering if any further natural process was about to be enacted. Perhaps Indaba-zimbi was going to fall to dust before my eyes. As I watched I observed that the discoloration was beginning to fade. First it vanished from the extremities, then from the larger limbs, and lastly from the trunk. Then in turn came the third stage of relaxation, the second stage of stiffness or rigor, and the first stage of after-death collapse. When all these had rapidly succeeded each other, Indaba-zimbi quietly woke up.

I was too astonished to speak; I simply looked at him with my mouth open.

"Well, Macumazahn," he said, putting his head on one side like a bird, and nodding his white lock in a comical fashion, "it is all right; I have seen her."

"Seen who?" I said.

"The Star, your wife, and the little maid. They are much frightened, but unharmed. The Babyan-frau watches them. She is mad, but the baboons obey her, and do not hurt them. The Star was sleeping from weariness, so I whispered in her ear and told her not to be frightened, for you would soon rescue her, and that meanwhile she must seem to be pleased to have Hendrika near her."

"You whispered in her ear?" I said. "How could you whisper in her ear?"

"Bah! Macumazahn. How could I seem to die and go rotten before your eyes? You don't know, do you? Well, I will tell you one thing. I had to die to pass the doors of space, as you call them. I had to draw all the healthy strength and life from my body in order to gather power to speak with the Star. It was a dangerous business, Macumazahn, for if I had let things go a little further they must have stopped so, and there would have been an end of Indaba-zimbi. Ah, you white men, you know so much that you think you know everything. But you don't! You are always staring at the clouds and can't see the things that lie at your feet. You hardly believe me now, do you, Macumazahn? Well, I will show you. Have you anything on you that the Star has touched or worn?"

I thought for a moment, and said that I had a lock of her hair in my pocket-book. He told me to give it him. I did so. Going to the fire, he lit the lock of hair in the flame, and let it burn to ashes, which he caught in his left hand. These ashes he mixed up in a paste with the juice of one of the leaves of the plant I have spoken of.

"Now, Macumazahn, shut your eyes," he said.

I did so, and he rubbed his paste on to my eyelids. At first it burnt me, then my head swam strangely. Presently this effect passed off, and my brain was perfectly clear again, but I could not feel the ground with my feet. Indaba-zimbi led me to the side of the stream. Beneath us was a pool of beautifully clear water.

"Look into the pool, Macumazahn," said Indaba-zimbi, and his voice sounded hollow and far away in my ears.

I looked. The water grew dark; it cleared, and in it was a picture. I saw a cave with a fire burning in it. Against the wall of the cave rested Stella. Her dress was torn almost off her, she looked dreadfully pale and weary, and her eyelids were red as though with weeping. But she slept, and I could almost think that I saw her lips shape my name in her sleep. Close to her, her head upon Stella's breast, was little Tota; she had a skin thrown over her to keep out the night cold. The child was awake, and appeared to be moaning with fear. By the fire, and in such a

169

position that the light fell full upon her face, and engaged in cooking something in a rough pot shaped from wood, sat the Baboon-woman, Hendrika. She was clothed in baboon skins, and her face had been rubbed with some dark stain, which was, however, wearing off it. In the intervals of her cooking she would turn on Stella her wild eyes, in which glared visible madness, with an expression of tenderness that amounted to worship. Then she would stare at the child and gnash her teeth as though with hate. Clearly she was jealous of it. Round the entrance arch of the cave peeped and peered the heads of many baboons. Presently Hendrika made a sign to one of them; apparently she did not speak, or rather grunt, in order not to wake Stella. The brute hopped forward, and she gave it a second rude wooden pot which was lying by her. It took it and went. The last thing that I saw, as the vision slowly vanished from the pool, was the dim shadow of the baboon returning with the pot full of water.

Presently everything had gone. I ceased to feel strange. There beneath me was the pool, and at my side stood Indaba-zimbi, smiling.

"You have seen things," he said.

"I have," I answered, and made no further remark on the matter. What was there to say?[*] "Do you know the path to the cave?" I added.

[*] For some almost equally remarkable instances of Kaffir magic the reader is referred to a work named "Among the

Zulus," by David Leslie.--Editor.

He nodded his head. "I did not follow it all just now, because it winds," he said. "But I know it. We shall want the ropes."

"Then let us be starting; the men have eaten."

He nodded his head again, and going to the men I told them to make ready, adding that Indaba-zimbi knew the way. They said that was all right, if Indaba-zimbi had "smelt her out," they should soon find the Star. So we started cheerfully enough, and my spirits were so much improved that I was able to eat a boiled mealie cob or two as we walked.

We went up the valley, following the course of the stream for about a mile; then Indaba-zimbi made a sudden turn to the right, along another kloof, of which there were countless numbers in the base of the great hill.

On we went through kloof after kloof. Indaba-zimbi, who led us, was never at a loss, he turned up gulleys and struck across necks of hills with the certainty of a hound on a hot scent. At length, after about three hours' march, we came to a big silent valley on the northern slope of the great peak. On one side of this valley was a series of stony koppies, on the other rose a sheer wall of rock. We marched along the wall for a distance of some two miles. Then suddenly Indaba-zimbi halted.

171

"There is the place," he said, pointing to an opening in the cliff. This
opening was about forty feet from the ground, and ellipse-shaped.
It cannot have been more than twenty feet high by ten wide, and was
partially hidden by ferns and bushes that grew about it in the surface
of the cliff. Keen as my eyes were, I doubt if I should ever have
noticed it, for there were many such cracks and crannies in the rocky
face of the great mountain.

We drew near and looked carefully at the place. The first thing I
noticed was that the rock, which was not quite perpendicular, had been
worn by the continual passage of baboons; the second, that something
white was hanging on a bush near the top of the ascent.

It was a pocket-handkerchief.

Now there was no more doubt about the matter. With a beating heart I
began the ascent. For the first twenty feet it was comparatively easy,
for the rock shelved; the next ten feet was very difficult, but still
possible to an active man, and I achieved it, followed by Indaba-zimbi.
But the last twelve or fifteen feet could only be scaled by throwing a
rope over the trunk of a stunted tree, which grew at the bottom of the
opening. This we accomplished with some trouble, and the rest was easy.
A foot or two above my head the handkerchief fluttered in the wind.
Hanging to the rope, I grasped it. It was my wife's. As I did so I
noticed the face of a baboon peering at me over the edge of the cleft,

the first baboon we had seen that morning. The brute gave a bark and vanished. Thrusting the handkerchief into my breast, I set my feet against the cliff and scrambled up as hard as I could go. I knew that we had no time to lose, for the baboon would quickly alarm the others. I gained the cleft. It was a mere arched passage cut by water, ending in a gulley, which led to a wide open space of some sort. I looked through the passage and saw that the gulley was black with baboons. On they came by the hundred. I unslung my elephant gun from my shoulders and waited, calling to the men below to come up with all possible speed. The brutes streamed on down the gloomy gulf towards me, barking, grunting, and showing their huge teeth. I waited till they were within fifteen yards. Then I fired the elephant gun, which was loaded with slugs, right into the thick of them. In that narrow place the report echoed like a cannon shot, but its sound was quickly swallowed in the volley of piercing human-sounding groans and screams that followed. The charge of heavy slugs had ploughed through the host of baboons, of which at least a dozen lay dead or dying in the passage. For a moment they hesitated, then they came on again with a hideous clamour. Fortunately by this time Indaba-zimbi, who also had a gun, was standing by my side, otherwise I should have been torn to pieces before I could re-load. He fired both barrels into them, and again checked the rush. But they came on again, and notwithstanding the appearance of two other natives with guns, which they let off with more or less success, we should have been overwhelmed by the great and ferocious apes had I not by this time succeeded in re-loading the elephant gun. When they were right on us, I fired, with even more deadly effect than before, for at that distance every slug

173

told on their long line. The howls and screams of pain and rage were now something inconceivable. One might have thought that we were doing battle with a host of demons; indeed in that light--for the overhanging arch of rock made it very dark--the gnashing snouts and sombre glowing eyes of the apes looked like those of devils as they are represented by monkish fancy. But the last shot was too much for them; they withdrew, dragging some of their wounded with them, and thus gave us time to get our men up the cliff. In a few minutes all were there, and we advanced down the passage, which presently opened into a rocky gulley with shelving sides. This gulley had a water-way at the bottom of it; it was about a hundred yards long, and the slopes on either side were topped by precipitous cliffs. I looked at these slopes; they literally swarmed with baboons, grunting, barking, screaming, and beating their breasts with their long arms, in fury. I looked up the water-way; along it, accompanied by a mob, or, as it were, a guard of baboons, ran Hendrika, her long hair flying, madness written on her face, and in her arms was the senseless form of little Tota.

She saw us, and a foam of rage burst from her lips. She screamed aloud. To me the sound was a mere inarticulate cry, but the baboons clearly understood it, for they began to roll rocks down on to us. One boulder leaped past me and struck down a Kaffir behind; another fell from the roof of the arch on to a man's head and killed him. Indaba-zimbi lifted his gun to shoot Hendrika; I knocked it up, so that the shot went over her, crying that he would kill the child. Then I shouted to the men to open out and form a line from side to side of the shelving gulley.

Furious at the loss of their two comrades, they obeyed me, and keeping in the water-way myself, together with Indaba-zimbi and the other guns, I gave the word to charge.

Then the real battle began. It is difficult to say who fought the most fiercely, the natives or the baboons. The Kaffirs charged along the slopes, and as they came, encouraged by the screams of Hendrika, who rushed to and fro holding the wretched Tota before her as a shield, the apes bounded at them in fury. Scores were killed by the assegais, and many more fell beneath our gun-shots; but still they came on. Nor did we go scathless. Occasionally a man would slip, or be pulled over in the grip of a baboon. Then the others would fling themselves upon him like dogs on a rat, and worry him to death. We lost five men in this way, and I myself received a bite through the fleshy part of the left arm, but fortunately a native near me assegaied the animal before I was pulled down.

At length, and all of a sudden, the baboons gave up. A panic seemed to seize them. Notwithstanding the cries of Hendrika they thought no more of fight, but only of escape; some even did not attempt to get away from the assegais of the Kaffirs, they simply hid their horrible faces in their paws, and, moaning piteously, waited to be slain.

Hendrika saw that the battle was lost. Dropping the child from her arms, she rushed straight at us, a very picture of horrible insanity. I lifted my gun, but could not bear to shoot. After all she was but a mad thing, half ape, half woman. So I sprang to one side, and she landed full on Indaba-zimbi, knocking him down. But she did not stay to do any more. Wailing terribly, she rushed down the gulley and through the arch, followed by a few of the surviving baboons, and vanished from our sight.

CHAPTER XIII

WHAT HAPPENED TO STELLA

The fight was over. In all we had lost seven men killed, and several
more severely bitten, while but few had escaped without some tokens
whereby he might remember what a baboon's teeth and claws are like. How
many of the brutes we killed I never knew, because we did not count, but
it was a vast number. I should think that the stock must have been low
about Babyan's Peak for many years afterwards. From that day to this,
however, I have always avoided baboons, feeling more afraid of them than
any beast that lives.

The path was clear, and we rushed forward along the water-course. But
first we picked up little Tota. The child was not in a swoon, as I had
thought, but paralyzed by terror, so that she could scarcely speak.
Otherwise she was unhurt, though it took her many a week to recover her
nerve. Had she been older, and had she not remembered Hendrika, I doubt
if she would have recovered it. She knew me again, and flung her little
arms about my neck, clinging to me so closely that I did not dare to
give her to any one else to carry lest I should add to her terrors. So I
went on with her in my arms. The fears that pierced my heart may well be
imagined. Should I find Stella living or dead? Should I find her at all?
Well, we should soon know now. We stumbled on up the stony watercourse;
notwithstanding the weight of Tota I led the way, for suspense lent me
wings. Now we were through, and an extraordinary scene lay before us. We

177

were in a great natural amphitheatre, only it was three times the size of any amphitheatre ever shaped by man, and the walls were formed of precipitous cliffs, ranging from one to two hundred feet in height. For the rest, the space thus enclosed was level, studded with park-like trees, brilliant with flowers, and having a stream running through the centre of it, that, as I afterwards discovered, welled up from the ground at the head of the open space.

We spread ourselves out in a line, searching everywhere, for Tota was too overcome to be able to tell us where Stella was hidden away. For nearly half an hour we searched and searched, scanning the walls of rock for any possible openings to a cave. In vain, we could find none. I applied to old Indaba-zimbi, but his foresight was at fault here. All he could say was that this was the place, and that the "Star" was hidden somewhere in a cave, but where the cave was he could not tell. At last we came to the top of the amphitheatre. There before us was a wall of rock, of which the lower parts were here and there clothed in grasses, lichens, and creepers. I walked along it, calling at the top of my voice.

Presently my heart stood still, for I thought I heard a faint answer. I drew nearer to the place from which the sound seemed to come, and again called. Yes, there was an answer in my wife's voice. It seemed to come from the rock. I went up to it and searched among the creepers, but still could find no opening.

"Move the stone," cried Stella's voice, "the cave is shut with a stone."

I took a spear and prodded at the cliff whence the sound came. Suddenly
the spear sunk in through a mass of lichen. I swept the lichen aside,
revealing a boulder that had been rolled into the mouth of an opening in
the rock, which it fitted so accurately that, covered as it was by
the overhanging lichen, it might well have escaped the keenest eye. We
dragged the boulder out; it was two men's work to do it. Beyond was
a narrow, water-worn passage, which I followed with a beating heart.
Presently the passage opened into a small cave, shaped like a pickle
bottle, and coming to a neck at the top end. We passed through and found
ourselves in a second, much larger cave, that I at once recognized as
the one of which Indaba-zimbi had shown me a vision in the water. Light
reached it from above--how I know not--and by it I could see a form
half-sitting, half lying on some skins at the top end of the cave. I
rushed to it. It was Stella! Stella bound with strips of hide, bruised,
torn, but still Stella, and alive.

She saw me, she gave one cry, then, as I caught her in my arms, she
fainted. It was happy indeed that she did not faint before, for had it
not been for the sound of her voice I do not believe we should ever have
found that cunningly hidden cave, unless, indeed, Indaba-zimbi's magic
(on which be blessings) had come to our assistance.

We bore her to the open air, laid her beneath the shade of a tree, and
cut the bonds loose from her ankles. As we went I glanced at the cave.

179

It was exactly as I had seen it in the vision. There burnt the fire, there were the rude wooden vessels, one of them still half full of the water which I had seen the baboon bring. I felt awed as I looked, and marvelled at the power wielded by a savage who could not even read and write.

Now I could see Stella clearly. Her face was scratched, and haggard with fear and weeping, her clothes were almost torn off her, and her beautiful hair was loose and tangled. I sent for water, and we sprinkled her face. Then I forced a little of the brandy which we distilled from peaches at the kraals between her lips, and she opened her eyes, and throwing her arms about me clung to me as little Tota had done, sobbing, "Thank God! thank God!"

After a while she grew quieter, and I made her and Tota eat some food from the store that we had brought with us. I too ate and was thankful, for with the exception of the mealie cobs I had tasted nothing for nearly four-and-twenty hours. Then she washed her face and hands, and tidied her rags of dress as well as she was able. As she did so by degrees I drew her story from her.

It seemed that on the previous afternoon, being wearied with packing, she went out to visit her father's grave, taking Tota with her, and was followed there by the two dogs. She wished to lay some flowers on the grave and take farewell of the dust it covered, for as we had expected to trek early on the morrow she did not know if she would find a later

180

opportunity. They passed up the garden, and gathering some flowers from the orange trees and elsewhere, went on to the little graveyard. Here she laid them on the grave as we had found them, and then sitting down, fell into a deep and sad reverie, such as the occasion would naturally induce. While she sat thus, Tota, who was a lively child and active as a kitten, strayed away without Stella observing it. With her went the dogs, who also had grown tired of inaction; a while passed, and suddenly she heard the dogs barking furiously about a hundred and fifty yards away. Then she heard Tota scream, and the dogs also yelling with fear and pain. She rose and ran as swiftly as she could towards the spot whence the sound came. Presently she was there. Before her in the glade, holding the screaming Tota in her arms, was a figure in which, notwithstanding the rough disguise of baboon skins and colouring matter, she had no difficulty in recognizing Hendrika, and all about her were numbers of baboons, rolling over and over in two hideous heaps, of which the centres were the unfortunate dogs now in process of being rent to fragments.

"Hendrika," Stella cried, "what does this mean? What are you doing with Tota and those brutes?"

The woman heard her and looked up. Then Stella saw that she was mad; madness stared from her eyes. She dropped the child, which instantly flew to Stella for protection. Stella clasped it, only to be herself clasped by Hendrika. She struggled fiercely, but it was of no use--the Babyan-frau had the strength of ten. She lifted her and Tota as though

they were nothing, and ran off with them, following the bed of the
stream in order to avoid leaving a spoor. Only the baboons who came with
her, minus the one the dogs had killed, would not take to the water, but
kept pace with them on the bank.

Stella said that the night which followed was more like a hideous
nightmare than a reality. She was never able to tell me all that
occurred in it. She had a vague recollection of being borne over rocks
and along kloofs, while around her echoed the horrible grunts and clicks
of the baboons. She spoke to Hendrika in English and Kaffir, imploring
her to let them go; but the woman, if I may call her so, seemed in her
madness to have entirely forgotten these tongues. When Stella spoke she
would kiss her and stroke her hair, but she did not seem to understand
what it was she said. On the other hand, she could, and did, talk to
the baboons, that seemed to obey her implicitly. Moreover, she would not
allow them to touch either Stella or the child in her arms. Once one
of them tried to do so, and she seized a dead stick and struck it
so heavily on the head that it fell senseless. Thrice Stella made an
attempt to escape, for sometimes even Hendrika's giant strength waned
and she had to set them down. But on each occasion she caught them, and
it was in these struggles that Stella's clothes were so torn. At length
before daylight they reached the cliff, and with the first break of
light the ascent began. Hendrika dragged them up the first stages, but
when they came to the precipitous place she tied the strips of hide,
of which she had a supply wound round her waist, beneath Stella's arms.
Steep as the place was the baboons ascended it easily enough, springing

from a knock of rock to the trunk of the tree that grew on the edge of the crevasse. Hendrika followed them, holding the end of the hide reim in her teeth, one of the baboons hanging down from the tree to assist her ascent. It was while she was ascending that Stella bethought of letting fall her handkerchief in the faint hope that some searcher might see it.

By this time Hendrika was on the tree, and grunting out orders to the baboons which clustered about Stella below. Suddenly these seized her and little Tota who was in her arms, and lifted her from the ground. Then Hendrika above, aided by other baboons, put out all her great strength and pulled the two of them up the rock. Twice Stella swung heavily against the cliff. After the second blow she felt her senses going, and was consumed with terror lest she should drop Tota. But she managed to cling to her, and together they reached the cleft.

"From that time," Stella went on, "I remember no more till I woke to find myself in a gloomy cave resting on a bed of skins. My legs were bound, and Hendrika sat near me watching me, while round the edge of the cave peered the heads of those horrible baboons. Tota was still in my arms, and half dead from terror; her moans were pitiful to hear. I spoke to Hendrika, imploring her to release us; but either she has lost all understanding of human speech, or she pretends to have done so. All she would do was to caress me, and even kiss my hands and dress with extravagant signs of affection. As she did so, Tota shrunk closer to me. This Hendrika saw and glared so savagely at the child that I feared lest she was going to kill her. I diverted her attention by making signs that I wanted water, and this she gave me in a wooden bowl. As you saw, the cave was evidently Hendrika's dwelling-place. There are stores of fruit in it and some strips of dried flesh. She gave me some of the fruit and Tota a little, and I made Tota eat some. You can never know what I went through, Allan. I saw now that Hendrika was quite mad, and but little removed from the brutes to which she is akin, and over which she has such unholy power. The only trace of humanity left about her was her affection for me. Evidently her idea was to keep me here with her, to keep me away from you, and to carry out this idea she was capable of the exercise of every artifice and cunning. In this way she was sane enough, but in every other way she was mad. Moreover, she had not forgotten her horrible jealousy. Already I saw her glaring at Tota, and knew that the child's murder was only a matter of time. Probably within a few hours she would be killed before my eyes. Of escape, even if I had the strength, there was absolutely no chance, and little enough of our ever being found. No, we should be kept here guarded by a mad thing, half ape, half woman, till we perished miserably. Then I thought of you, dear, and of all that you must be suffering, and my heart nearly broke. I could only pray to God that I might either be rescued or die swiftly.

"As I prayed I dropped into a kind of doze from utter weariness, and then I had the strangest dream. I dreamed that Indaba-zimbi stood over me nodding his white lock, and spoke to me in Kaffir, telling me not to be frightened, for you would soon be with me, and that meanwhile I must humour Hendrika, pretending to be pleased to have her near me. The dream

184

was so vivid that I actually seemed to see and hear him, as I see and hear him now."

Here I looked up and glanced at old Indaba-zimbi, who was sitting near. But it was not till afterwards that I told Stella of how her vision was brought about.

"At any rate," she went on, "when I awoke I determined to act on my dream. I took Hendrika's hand, and pressed it. She actually laughed in a wild kind of way with happiness, and laid her head upon my knee. Then I made signs that I wanted food, and she threw wood on the fire, which I forgot to tell you was burning in the cave, and began to make some of the broth that she used to cook very well, and she did not seem to have forgotten all about it. At any rate the broth was not bad, though neither Tota nor I could drink much of it. Fright and weariness had taken away our appetites.

"After the meal was done--and I prolonged it as much as possible--I saw Hendrika was beginning to get jealous of Tota again. She glared at her and then at the big knife which was tied round her own body. I knew the knife again, it was the one with which she had tried to murder you, dear. At last she went so far as to draw the knife. I was paralyzed with fear, then suddenly I remembered that when she was our servant, and used to get out of temper and sulk, I could always calm her by singing to her. So I began to sing hymns. Instantly she forgot her jealousy and put the knife back into its sheath. She knew the sound of the singing, and

185

sat listening to it with a rapt face; the baboons, too, crowded in at the entrance of the cave to listen. I must have sung for an hour or more, all the hymns that I could remember. It was so very strange and dreadful sitting there singing to mad Hendrika and those hideous man-like apes that shut their eyes and nodded their great heads as I sang. It was a horrible nightmare; but I believe that the baboons are almost as human as the Bushmen.

"Well, this went on for a long time till my voice was getting exhausted. Then suddenly I heard the baboons outside raise a loud noise, as they do when they are angry. Then, dear, I heard the boom of your elephant gun, and I think it was the sweetest sound that ever came to my ears. Hendrika heard it too. She sprang up, stood for a moment, then, to my horror, swept Tota into her arms and rushed down the cave. Of course I could not stir to follow her, for my feet were tied. Next instant I heard the sound of a rock being moved, and presently the lessening of the light in the cave told me that I was shut in. Now the sound even of the elephant gun only reached me very faintly, and presently I could hear nothing more, straining my ears as I would.

"At last I heard a faint shouting that reached me through the wall of rock. I answered as loud as I could. You know the rest; and oh, my dear husband, thank God! thank God!" and she fell weeping into my arms.

CHAPTER XIV

FIFTEEN YEARS AFTER

Both Stella and Tota were too weary to be moved, so we camped that night in the baboons' home, but were troubled by no baboons. Stella would not sleep in the cave; she said the place terrified her, so I made her up a kind of bed under a thorn-tree. As this rock-bound valley was one of the hottest places I ever was in, I thought that this would not matter; but when at sunrise on the following morning I saw a veil of miasmatic mist hanging over the surface of the ground, I changed my opinion. However, neither Stella nor Tota seemed the worse, so as soon as was practical we started homewards. I had already on the previous day sent some of the men back to the kraals to fetch a ladder, and when we reached the cliff we found them waiting for us beneath. With the help of the ladder the descent was easy. Stella simply got out of her rough litter at the top of the cliff, for we found it necessary to carry her, climbed down the ladder, and got into it again at the bottom.

Well, we reached the kraals safely enough, seeing nothing more of Hendrika, and, were this a story, doubtless I should end it here with--"and lived happily ever after." But alas! it is not so. How am I to write it?

My dearest wife's vital energy seemed completely to fail her now that the danger was past, and within twelve hours of our return I saw that

her state was such as to necessitate the abandonment of any idea of
leaving Babyan Kraals at present. The bodily exertion, the anguish of
mind, and the terror which she had endured during that dreadful night,
combined with her delicate state of health, had completely broken her
down. To make matters worse, also, she was taken with an attack of
fever, contracted no doubt in the unhealthy atmosphere of that accursed
valley. In time she shook the fever off, but it left her dreadfully
weak, and quite unfit to face the trial before her.

I think she knew that she was going to die; she always spoke of my
future, never of our future. It is impossible for me to tell how sweet
she was; how gentle, how patient and resigned. Nor, indeed, do I wish
to tell it, it is too sad. But this I will say, I believe that if ever
a woman drew near to perfection while yet living on the earth, Stella
Quatermain did so.

The fatal hour drew on. My boy Harry was born, and his mother lived
to kiss and bless him. Then she sank. We did what we could, but we had
little skill, and might not hold her back from death. All through one
weary night I watched her with a breaking heart.

The dawn came, the sun rose in the east. His rays falling on the peak
behind were reflected in glory upon the bosom of the western sky. Stella
awoke from her swoon and saw the light. She whispered to me to open the
door of the hut. I did so, and she fixed her dying eyes on the splendour
of the morning sky. She looked on me and smiled as an angel might

188

smile. Then with a last effort she lifted her hand, and, pointing to the radiant heavens, whispered:

"There, Allan, there!"

It was done, and I was broken-hearted, and broken-hearted I must wander to the end. Those who have endured my loss will know my sorrow; it cannot be written. In such peace and at such an hour may I also die!

Yes, it is a sad story, but wander where we will about the world we can never go beyond the sound of the passing bell. For me, as for my father before me, and for the millions who have been and who shall be, there is but one word of comfort. "The Lord hath given, and the Lord hath taken away." Let us, then, bow our heads in hope, and add with a humble heart, "Blessed be the name of the Lord."

I buried her by her father's side, and the weeping of the people who had loved her went up to heaven. Even Indaba-zimbi wept, but I could weep no more.

On the second night from her burial I could not sleep. I rose, dressed myself, and went out into the night. The moon was shining brightly, and by its rays I shaped my course towards the graveyard. I drew near silently, and as I came I thought that I heard a sound of moaning on the

189

further side of the wall. I looked over it. Crouched by Stella's grave, and tearing at its sods with her hands, as though she would unearth that which lay within, was Hendrika. Her face was wild and haggard, her form was so emaciated that when the pelts she wore slipped aside, the shoulder-blades seemed to project almost through her skin. Suddenly she looked up and saw me. Laughing a dreadful maniac laugh, she put her hand to her girdle and drew her great knife from it. I thought that she was about to attack me, and prepared to defend myself as I best could, for I was unarmed. But she made no effort to do so. Lifting the knife on high, for a moment she held it glittering in the moonlight, then plunged it into her own breast, and fell headlong to the ground.

I sprang over the wall and ran to her. She was not yet dead. Presently she opened her eyes, and I saw that the madness had gone out of them.

"Macumazahn," she said, speaking in English and in an thick difficult voice like one who half forgot and half remembered--"Macumazahn, I remember now. I have been mad. Is she really dead, Macumazahn?"

"Yes," I said, "she is dead, and you killed her."

"I killed her!" the dying woman faltered, "and I loved her. Yes, yes, I know now. I became a brute again and dragged her to the brutes, and now once more I am a woman, and she is dead, and I killed her--because I loved her so. I killed her who saved me from the brutes. I am not dead yet, Macumazahn. Take me and torture me to death, slowly, very slowly.

190

It was jealousy of you that drove me mad, and I have killed her, and now she never can forgive me."

"Ask forgiveness from above," I said, for Hendrika had been a Christian, and the torment of her remorse touched me.

"I ask no forgiveness," she said. "May God torture me for ever, because I killed her; may I become a brute for ever till she comes to find me and forgives me! I only want her forgiveness." And wailing in an anguish of the heart so strong that her bodily suffering seemed to be forgotten, Hendrika, the Baboon-woman, died.

I went back to the kraals, and, waking Indaba-zimbi, told him what had happened, asking him to send some one to watch the body, as I proposed to give it burial. But next morning it was gone, and I found that the natives, hearing of the event, had taken the corpse and thrown it to the vultures with every mark of hate. Such, then, was the end of Hendrika.

A week after Hendrika's death I left Babyan Kraals. The place was hateful to me now; it was a haunted place. I sent for old Indaba-zimbi and told him that I was going. He answered that it was well. "The place has served your turn," he said; "here you have won that joy which it was fated you should win, and have suffered those things that it was fated you should suffer. Yes, and though you know it not now, the joy and the suffering, like the sunshine and the storm, are the same thing, and will rest at last in the same heaven, the heaven from which they came. Now go, Macumazahn."

I asked him if he was coming with me.

"No," he answered, "our paths lie apart henceforth, Macumazahn. We met together for certain ends. Those ends are fulfilled. Now each one goes his own way. You have still many years before you, Macumazahn; my years are few. When we shake hands here it will be for the last time. Perhaps we may meet again, but it will not be in this world. Henceforth we have each of us a friend the less."

"Heavy words," I said.

"True words," he answered.

Well, I have little heart to write the rest of it. I went, leaving Indaba-zimbi in charge of the place, and making him a present of such cattle and goods as I did not want.

Tota, I of course took with me. Fortunately by this time she had almost recovered the shock to her nerves. The baby Harry, as he was afterwards named, was a fine healthy child, and I was lucky in getting a respectable native woman, whose husband had been killed in the fight with the baboons, to accompany me as his nurse.

Slowly, and followed for a distance by all the people, I trekked away from Babyan Kraals. My route towards Natal was along the edge of the Bad Lands, and my first night's outspan was beneath that very tree where Stella, my lost wife, had found us as we lay dying of thirst.

I did not sleep much that night. And yet I was glad that I had not died in the desert about eleven months before. I felt then, as from year to year I have continued to feel while I wander through the lonely wilderness of life, that I had been preserved to an end. I had won my darling's love, and for a little while we had been happy together. Our happiness was too perfect to endure. She is lost to me now, but she is lost to be found again.

Here on the following morning I bade farewell to Indaba-zimbi.

"Good-bye, Macumazahn," he said, nodding his white lock at me. "Good-bye for a while. I am not a Christian; your father could not make me that. But he was a wise man, and when he said that those who loved each other shall meet again, he did not lie. And I too am a wise man in my way, Macumazahn, and I say it is true that we shall meet again. All my prophecies to you have come true, Macumazahn, and this one shall come true also. I tell you that you shall return to Babyan Kraals and shall not find me. I tell you that you shall journey to a further land than Babyan Kraals and shall find me. Farewell!" and he took a pinch of snuff, turned, and went.

Of my journey down to Natal there is little to tell. I met with many adventures, but they were of an every-day kind, and in the end arrived safely at Port Durban, which I now visited for the first time. Both Tota and my baby boy bore the journey well. And here I may as well chronicle the destiny of Tota. For a year she remained under my charge. Then she was adopted by a lady, the wife of an English colonel, who was stationed at the Cape. She was taken by her adopted parents to England, where she grew up a very charming and pretty girl, and ultimately married a clergyman in Norfolk. But I never saw her again, though we often wrote to each other.

Before I returned to the country of my birth, she too had been gathered to the land of shadows, leaving three children behind her. Ah me! all this took place so long ago, when I was young who now am old.

Perhaps it may interest the reader to know the fate of Mr. Carson's property, which should of course have gone to his grandson Harry. I wrote to England to claim the estate on his behalf, but the lawyer to whom the matter was submitted said that my marriage to Stella, not having been celebrated by an ordained priest, was not legal according to English law, and therefore Harry could not inherit. Foolishly enough I acquiesced in this, and the property passed to a cousin of my father-in-law's; but since I have come to live in England I have been

informed that this opinion is open to great suspicion, and that there
is every probability that the courts would have declared the marriage
perfectly binding as having been solemnly entered into in accordance
with the custom of the place where it was contracted. But I am now so
rich that it is not worth while to move in the matter. The cousin is
dead, his son is in possession, so let him keep it.

Once, and once only, did I revisit Babyan Kraals. Some fifteen years
after my darling's death, when I was a man in middle life, I undertook
an expedition to the Zambesi, and one night outspanned at the mouth of
the well-known valley beneath the shadow of the great peak. I mounted
my horse, and, quite alone, rode up the valley, noticing with a strange
prescience of evil that the road was overgrown, and, save for the music
of the waterfalls, the place silent as death. The kraals that used to be
to the left of the road by the river had vanished. I rode towards their
site; the mealie fields were choked with weeds, the paths were dumb with
grass. Presently I reached the place. There, overgrown with grass, were
the burnt ashes of the kraals, and there among the ashes, gleaming in
the moonlight, lay the white bones of men. Now it was clear to me. The
settlement had been fallen on by some powerful foe, and its inhabitants
put to the assegai. The forebodings of the natives had come true; Babyan
Kraals were peopled by memories alone.

I passed on up the terraces. There shone the roofs of the marble huts.
They would not burn, and were too strong to be easily pulled down. I
entered one of them--it had been our sleeping hut--and lit a candle

which I had with me. The huts had been sacked; leaves of books and broken mouldering fragments of the familiar furniture lay about. Then I remembered that there was a secret place hollowed in the floor and concealed by a stone, where Stella used to hide her little treasures. I went to the stone and dragged it up. There was something within wrapped in rotting native cloth. I undid it. It was the dress my wife had been married in. In the centre of the dress were the withered wreath and flowers she had worn, and with them a little paper packet. I opened it; it contained a lock of my own hair!

I remembered then that I had searched for this dress when I came away and could not find it, for I had forgotten the secret recess in the floor.

Taking the dress with me, I left the hut for the last time. Leaving my horse tied to a tree, I walked to the graveyard, through the ruined garden. There it was a mass of weeds, but over my darling's grave grew a self-sown orange bush, of which the scented petals fell in showers on to the mound beneath. As I drew near, there was a crash and a rush. A great baboon leapt from the centre of the graveyard and vanished into the trees. I could almost believe that it was the wraith of Hendrika doomed to keep an eternal watch over the bones of the woman her jealous rage had done to death.

I tarried there a while, filled with such thoughts as may not be written. Then, leaving my dead wife to her long sleep where the waters

196

fall in melancholy music beneath the shadow of the everlasting mountain, I turned and sought that spot where first we had told our love. Now the orange grove was nothing but a tangled thicket; many of the trees were dead, choked with creepers, but some still flourished. There stood the one beneath which we had lingered, there was the rock that had been our seat, and there on the rock sat the wraith of Stella, the Stella whom I had wed! Ay! there she sat, and on her upturned face was that same spiritual look which I saw upon it in the hour when we first had kissed. The moonlight shone in her dark eyes, the breeze wavered in her curling hair, her breast rose and fell, a gentle smile played about her parted lips. I stood transfixed with awe and joy, gazing on that lost loveliness which once was mine. I could not speak, and she spoke no word; she did not even seem to see me. Now her eyes fell. For a moment they met mine, and their message entered into me.

Then she was gone. She was gone; nothing was left but the tremulous moonlight falling where she had been, the melancholy music of the waters, the shadow of the everlasting mountain, and, in my heart, the sorrow and the hope.

Made in the USA
Middletown, DE
11 December 2015